D1281095

Better Homes and Gardens®

SOUPS & STEWS

First Edition. First Printing.
Library of Congress Catalog Card Number: 86-62163
ISBN: 0-696-02203-6

Soups and Stews
Editor Joyce Trollope
Copy and Production Editor Mary Helen Schiltz
Graphic Designer Harijs Priekulis
Electronic Text Processor Donna Russell
Photographers Michael Jensen and Sean Fitzgerald
Food Stylists Suzanne Finley, Dianna Nolin, Janet Pittman, Maria Rolandelli

On the cover
Country-Style Pork Stew (see recipe, page 90)

Our seal assures you that every recipe in *Soups and Stews* has been tested in the Better Homes and Gardens® Test Kitchen. This means that each recipe is practical and reliable, and meets our high standards of taste appeal.

Three cheers for soups and stews. Easy! . . . Nourishing! . . . Delicious! These outstanding qualities fit the recipes you'll find throughout *Soups and Stews.*

How easy? Our book unlocks the secret of making satisfying homemade soups without difficulty. The key to effortless soups and stews is simple scratch cooking or stir-together convenience. Even meal planning becomes a snap when you serve soup. Add crusty bread or crisp crackers and a fresh salad for a meal that's easy on the cook.

You'll find our homemade soup and stew combinations are nourishing, too. Many are packed with meats, vegetables, and juices that are downright good for you!

But, most important, the soup and stew recipes you'll prepare are delicious and full of tantalizing flavors. Get ready to tempt your taste buds and satisfy your hunger because you're in for some mighty good sippin' spoonfuls.

Contents

Heat-and-Serve Soups

When you're short on time, stir together a quick, whole-meal soup. Do you need some luscious, mouth-watering suggestions? Check the next few pages for our favorite speedy-soup nominations. These streamlined, meal-in-a-dish soups require less than 25 minutes from start to finish!

Corn and Broccoli Chowder

Corn and Broccoli Chowder

1 10-ounce package frozen cut broccoli
1 6-ounce package sliced fully cooked ham
1 10¾-ounce can condensed cream of onion soup
1 soup can (1¼ cups) milk
1 8½-ounce can cream-style corn
½ teaspoon dried thyme, crushed
½ of a 4-ounce package (½ cup) shredded cheddar cheese
Carrot sticks (optional)

In a large saucepan combine broccoli and ½ cup *water*. Bring to boiling. Reduce heat, then simmer, covered, for 5 minutes or till broccoli is just tender. *Do not* drain.

Meanwhile, cut ham into thin strips measuring 2x¼ inches (see photo 1). Set aside. Stir soup, milk, *undrained* corn, and thyme into broccoli (see photo 2). Bring to boiling. Reduce heat, then simmer, covered, about 1 minute or till heated through (see photo 3). Stir in ham and heat for 1 to 2 minutes or till hot. Ladle into soup bowls or heat-proof mugs (see photo 4). Sprinkle with cheese. Serve with carrot sticks, if desired. Makes 3 main-dish servings.

2 Carefully stir the condensed soup, milk, corn, and thyme into the cooked broccoli in the saucepan. Use a gentle stirring action so the broccoli stays in bite-size pieces. Stirring too vigorously breaks the broccoli into tiny pieces.

1 Quickly cut food by stacking it on a cutting board. Use a sharp knife to cut through all the layers at once, cutting to the desired dimensions. A few quick cuts slice the entire package.

3 After you bring the mixture to boiling, reduce the heat so the soup is just simmering. Simmering is when a few bubbles form slowly and burst just before they reach the surface. Cover the soup and let it simmer just till it is heated through.

4 To serve the soup, use a deep ladle to spoon the soup into soup bowls or heat-proof mugs. Then sprinkle a little cheese atop each serving.

Sausage-Bean Soup

Just quickly heat everything together for a tasty bean-and-bacon soup fix-up.

8 ounces fully cooked Polish sausage
2 cups water
1 10-ounce package frozen mixed vegetables
1 tablespoon dried minced onion
1 tablespoon dried chopped green pepper
1 11½-ounce can condensed bean with bacon soup
Grated Parmesan cheese (optional)

Cut sausage into thin slices; set aside. In a large saucepan combine water, frozen mixed vegetables, dried onion, and dried green pepper. Bring to boiling. Reduce heat, then simmer, covered, about 5 minutes or till vegetables are just tender. *Do not* drain.

Stir in sausage slices and condensed bean with bacon soup. Bring mixture to boiling. Reduce heat, then simmer, covered, about 1 minute or till mixture is heated through (see photo 3, page 8). Ladle into soup bowls (see photo 4, page 9). If desired, sprinkle with grated Parmesan cheese. Makes 4 main-dish servings.

Microwave Directions: Cut sausage into thin slices; set aside. In a 2-quart microwave-safe casserole combine *½ cup* of the water, frozen mixed vegetables, dried onion, and dried green pepper. Micro-cook, covered, on 100% power (HIGH) for 8 to 10 minutes or till vegetables are just tender. Stir in sausage, remaining water, and condensed bean with bacon soup. Micro-cook, uncovered, for 4 to 5 minutes or till heated through. Ladle into soup bowls (see photo 4, page 9). If desired, sprinkle with grated Parmesan cheese. Makes 4 main-dish servings.

Speedy Pastrami Chili

Only 5 ingredients plus a soup can of water make this soup so quick to fix.

4 ounces smoked turkey sausage links
2 11¼-ounce cans condensed chili beef soup
1 soup can (1¼ cups) water
¼ cup salsa
1 tablespoon dried minced onion
⅓ cup dairy sour cream

Cut sausage links in half lengthwise, then cut each half into ½-inch-thick pieces. In a large saucepan combine sliced sausage, condensed chili beef soup, water, salsa, and dried onion.

Bring soup mixture to boiling. Reduce heat, then simmer, uncovered, about 5 minutes or till heated through, stirring occasionally (see photo 3, page 8). Ladle into soup bowls (see photo 4, page 9). Dollop each serving with sour cream. Makes 3 main-dish servings.

Microwave Directions: Cut sausage links in half lengthwise, then cut each half into ½-inch-thick pieces. In a 1½-quart microwave-safe casserole combine sausage, condensed chili beef soup, water, salsa, and dried onion. Micro-cook, covered, on 100% power (HIGH) for 10 to 12 minutes or till heated through, stirring twice. Ladle into soup bowls (see photo 4, page 9). Dollop each serving with sour cream. Makes 3 main-dish servings.

Hot Tamale Stew

Skip the trip to Mexico. Instead, get south-of-the border flavor right here.

1 15-ounce can tamales
1 12-ounce can vegetable juice cocktail
1 8-ounce can red kidney beans, drained
1 7½-ounce can tomatoes, cut up
1 cup frozen whole kernel corn
½ cup water
1 teaspoon sugar
Several dashes bottled hot pepper sauce (optional)
Dash pepper
1 4-ounce package (1 cup) shredded mozzarella cheese

Drain tamales, reserving the liquid. Remove the paper from tamales. Stack the tamales and cut into ½-inch slices (see photo 1, page 8). In a large saucepan stir together sliced tamales; the reserved tamale liquid; vegetable juice cocktail; drained kidney beans; *undrained* tomatoes; corn; water; sugar; bottled hot pepper sauce, if desired; and pepper.

Bring to boiling. Reduce heat, then simmer, uncovered, for 5 minutes, stirring occasionally (see photo 3, page 8). Ladle into soup bowls (see photo 4, page 9). Sprinkle each serving with cheese. Makes 3 main-dish servings.

Microwave Directions: Drain tamales, reserving liquid. Remove paper from tamales. Stack the tamales and cut into ½-inch slices (see photo 1, page 8). In a 2-quart microwave-safe casserole combine sliced tamales; the reserved tamale liquid; vegetable juice cocktail; drained kidney beans; *undrained* tomatoes; corn; water; sugar; hot pepper sauce, if desired; and pepper. Micro-cook, covered, on 100% power (HIGH) for 10 to 12 minutes or till heated through, stirring twice. Ladle into soup bowls (see photo 4, page 9). Sprinkle each serving with cheese. Makes 3 main-dish servings.

Bratwurst-Macaroni Soup

No bratwurst in the refrigerator? Substitute 8 ounces of frankfurters for the sausage.

8 ounces smoked bratwurst links
1 3-serving-size envelope *regular* vegetable soup mix
1 7¼-ounce package macaroni-and-cheese mix
2½ cups water
1 teaspoon dried basil, crushed
⅛ teaspoon pepper
3 cups milk
Grated Parmesan cheese

Cut bratwurst links into thin slices; set aside. In a large saucepan combine soup mix and cheese sauce mix from the macaroni-and-cheese mix. Add water, basil, and pepper. Stir till combined.

Stir in uncooked macaroni. Bring to boiling. Reduce heat, then simmer, covered, for 7 to 10 minutes or till vegetables and macaroni are tender, stirring occasionally (see photo 3, page 8). Stir in milk and sausage; heat through. Ladle into soup bowls (see photo 4, page 9). Sprinkle with Parmesan cheese and serve immediately. Makes 4 main-dish servings.

Chilly No-Cook Soups

Too hot to cook? Make a cold, no-cook soup! It'll keep you and your kitchen "cool as a cucumber."

These soups need no heating—only a thorough chilling. Nobody takes the heat with our cold soups, least of all your kitchen.

So, sit back and keep your cool. Let each chilly sip refresh you.

Gazpacho

Gazpacho

A refreshing way to enjoy an abundant summer crop of tomatoes, cucumbers, and green peppers.

3 medium tomatoes
1 small cucumber, chopped
1 medium green pepper, chopped
2 green onions, sliced
1 clove garlic, minced
1 12-ounce can (1½ cups) vegetable juice cocktail
2 tablespoons vinegar
1 teaspoon olive oil *or* cooking oil
¼ teaspoon salt
¼ teaspoon dried basil, crushed
Several dashes bottled hot pepper sauce
Croutons (optional)

Peel tomatoes (see photo 1). Coarsely chop the tomatoes. In a large mixing bowl combine tomatoes, cucumber, green pepper, and green onions. Mince garlic (see photo 2). Stir the garlic, vegetable juice cocktail, vinegar, olive oil or cooking oil, salt, basil, and hot pepper sauce into the tomato mixture (see photo 3).

Cover and chill in the refrigerator for several hours or till thoroughly chilled (see photo 4). Ladle into soup bowls. Garnish with croutons, if desired. Makes 4 side-dish servings.

1 Carefully plunge the tomato into boiling water for 20 to 30 seconds to loosen the skin. Then, immediately immerse the tomato in cold water. With a knife, remove the loosened skin, or slip it off with your fingers.

Guacamole Soup

Get avocado flavor without the hassle of peeling and seeding fresh avocados. Just start with frozen dip.

1 large tomato
1 14½-ounce can chicken broth
1 6-ounce container frozen avocado dip, thawed
1 cup light cream *or* milk
2 tablespoons chopped canned green chili peppers
1 tablespoons lemon juice
2 teaspoons dried minced onion

Peel the tomato (see photo 1). Seed and chop the tomato (should have about 1 cup).

In a mixing bowl gradually stir broth into dip. Stir in tomato, cream or milk, chili peppers, lemon juice, and onion (see photo 3). Cover; chill in the refrigerator for several hours or till thoroughly chilled (see photo 4). Ladle into soup bowls. Makes 8 appetizer servings.

2 Instead of a garlic press, use a cutting board and a chef's knife. On the cutting board, press down and forward on the garlic with one flat side of the chef's knife till the garlic is flattened. Remove the peel. Cut the flattened garlic into very tiny pieces.

3 Throughly mix the ingredients together. Make sure the seasonings are evenly distributed so the flavors of the soup combine.

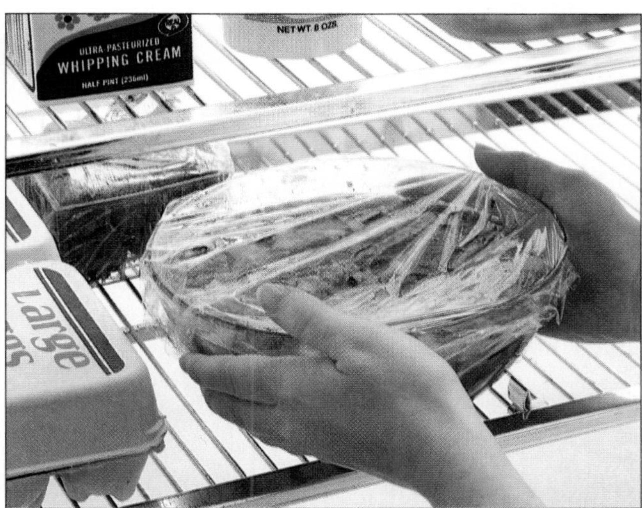

4 Cover the bowl with clear plastic wrap before chilling. A 1½-quart plastic storage container with a lid also makes a handy bowl for mixing and storing.

Pasta Soups From a Homemade Mix

Do-it-yourself! Make your own "souper-delicious" pasta soup mixes. These mixes give your soups a convenient head start.

Begin the home project by bagging a bunch of the pasta soup mixes all at once. Then, stash them away. You'll have homemade convenience right at your fingertips.

All that's left to do is turn the mix into one of our mouth-watering soups.

Ham-and-Spinach Soup

Pick-a-Pasta Make-Ahead Mix

Make 6 mixes at a time by measuring the ingredients, assembly-line fashion, into separate containers. You'll discover the time savings that come from having extra soup mixes on the shelf.

- **4 cups small pasta (elbow macaroni, bow ties, corkscrew macaroni, cavatelli, medium shells, *or* wagon-wheel macaroni)**
- **1½ cups dried chopped mushrooms (optional)**
- **6 tablespoons dried minced onion**
- **6 tablespoons instant chicken bouillon granules**
- **6 teaspoons dried parsley flakes**
- **½ teaspoon garlic powder**

Select the desired pasta (see photo 1). For each mix, in a plastic bag or airtight container combine *⅔ cup* pasta; *¼ cup* dried mushrooms, if desired; *1 tablespoon* dried onion; *1 tablespoon* bouillon granules; *1 teaspoon* dried parsley; and *dash* garlic powder (see photo 2). Store tightly sealed till needed (see photo 3). Makes 6 (¾- to 1-cup) portions.

Pick-a-Pasta Soup: To prepare soup, in a 2-quart saucepan stir together one portion Pick-a-Pasta Make-Ahead Mix, 3 cups *water,* and ½ teaspoon dried *oregano,* crushed. Bring to boiling. Reduce heat, then simmer, covered, for 7 to 12 minutes or till pasta is tender, stirring occasionally (see photo 4). Ladle soup into bowls. Sprinkle with grated *Parmesan cheese,* if desired. Makes 3 side-dish servings.

1 Choose a combination of small pasta shapes or all of one kind from those listed in the recipe. The pictures on the right help you identify the pasta shapes in the grocery store.

Elbow macaroni

Bow ties

Corkscrew macaroni

Cavatelli

Medium shells

Wagon-wheel macaroni

Ham-and-Spinach Soup

4 cups water
1 portion Pick-a-Pasta Make-Ahead Mix (see recipe, opposite)
1 cup diced fully cooked ham
1½ cups chopped fresh spinach (about 5 ounces)
¼ teaspoon dried oregano, crushed
Sieved hard-cooked egg (optional)
Grated Parmesan cheese (optional)

In a 2-quart saucepan combine water, soup mix, and ham. Bring to boiling. Reduce heat. Simmer, covered, for 7 to 12 minutes or till pasta is tender, stirring occasionally (see photo 4). Stir in spinach and oregano. Cover and cook about 2 minutes or till spinach is done. Ladle into soup bowls. If desired, garnish with egg or sprinkle with cheese. Makes 4 side-dish servings.

2 No need to use a bowl to combine the ingredients. Six plastic storage bags or containers fill the bill. Be sure to put each individual portion into its own bag or container. If you try to store the mix in bulk, the seasonings will settle to the bottom.

4 Remove a piece of the pasta near the end of the cooking time to test it for doneness. The pasta should be tender, but still slightly firm when taste-tested.

3 Before storing the mix, tightly seal each plastic bag or container. Then keep it on your cupboard shelf for up to six months without losing any flavor.

Corn-Pasta Chowder

2 cups water
1 portion Pick-a-Pasta Make-Ahead Mix (see recipe, page 18)
¼ teaspoon dried basil, crushed
1 17-ounce can cream-style corn
1 12-ounce can evaporated milk
1 3-ounce package sliced smoked beef, turkey, chicken, *or* ham, snipped

In a 2-quart saucepan combine water, soup mix, and basil. Bring to boiling. Reduce heat, then simmer, covered, for 7 to 12 minutes or till the pasta is tender, stirring occasionally (see photo 4, page 19). Stir in *undrained* cream-style corn, evaporated milk, and snipped beef, turkey, chicken, or ham. Cover and cook till heated through. Ladle into soup bowls. Makes 3 main-dish servings.

Chili-Bean Pasta Soup

It tastes like meatless chili!

2½ cups water
1 16-ounce can tomatoes, cut up
1 15½-ounce can chili beans
1 portion Pick-a-Pasta Make-Ahead Mix (see recipe, page 18)
1 teaspoon chili powder
Shredded cheddar cheese (optional)

In a 3-quart saucepan stir together water, *undrained* tomatoes, *undrained* chili beans, soup mix, and chili powder. Bring to boiling. Reduce heat, then simmer, covered, for 7 to 12 minutes or till pasta is tender, stirring occasionally (see photo 4, page 19). Ladle into soup bowls. If desired, sprinkle each serving with shredded cheddar cheese. Makes 6 side-dish servings.

Pepperoni-and-Vegetable Soup

3 cups water
1 12-ounce can (1½ cups) vegetable juice cocktail
1 10-ounce package frozen mixed vegetables
1 portion Pick-a-Pasta Make-Ahead Mix (see recipe, page 18)
½ teaspoon dried oregano, crushed
3½ ounces sliced pepperoni, halved
Grated Parmesan cheese

In a 3-quart saucepan combine water, vegetable juice cocktail, frozen mixed vegetables, soup mix, and oregano. Bring to boiling. Reduce heat, then simmer, covered, for 7 to 12 minutes or till pasta is tender, stirring occasionally (see photo 4, page 19). Stir in pepperoni. Cover and cook till heated through. Ladle into soup bowls. Sprinkle with Parmesan cheese. Makes 6 side-dish servings.

Pasta Nutrition

Pasta is a healthy choice for hungry people. Sometimes it's thought of as a fattening food. Not true! The rich sauces often added to pasta are where the calories lurk rather than in the pasta itself. One-half cup of cooked pasta averages about 100 calories. It also contributes protein, carbohydrates, and vitamins to our diets. And frequently, packaged pasta is even further enriched with thiamine, riboflavin, niacin, and iron.

Tuna-Rosemary Soup

3½ cups water
1 portion Pick-a-Pasta Make-Ahead Mix (see recipe, page 18)
1 cup frozen loose-pack cut green beans
¼ teaspoon dried rosemary, crushed
¼ teaspoon lemon pepper
1 6½-ounce can tuna, drained and broken into chunks, *or* one 7¾-ounce can salmon drained, flaked, and skin and bones removed
1 tablespoon chopped pimiento

In a 2-quart saucepan combine water, soup mix, frozen beans, rosemary, and lemon pepper. Bring to boiling. Reduce heat, then simmer, covered, for 7 to 12 minutes or till pasta is tender, stirring occasionally (see photo 4, page 19). Stir in tuna or salmon and pimiento. Cover and cook till heated through. Ladle into soup bowls. Makes 3 main-dish servings.

Pea Pod Appetizer Broth

Enoki mushrooms are tiny Japanese mushrooms available in the fresh produce section of large supermarkets.

3½ cups water
1 portion Pick-a-Pasta Make-Ahead Mix (see recipe, page 18)
⅛ teaspoon ground ginger
½ of a 6-ounce package frozen pea pods, halved crosswise
1 tablespoon soy sauce
Enoki mushrooms (optional)

In a 2-quart saucepan combine water, soup mix, and ground ginger. Bring to boiling. Reduce heat, then simmer, covered, for 7 to 12 minutes or till pasta is tender, stirring occasionally (see photo 4, page 19). Stir in pea pods and soy sauce. Cover and cook for 1 to 2 minutes or till heated through. Ladle into soup bowls. Garnish each serving with enoki mushrooms, if desired. Makes 4 appetizer servings.

Indonesian-Style Chicken Chowder

Curry flavor added to this creamy soup makes it reminiscent of Indonesian cuisine.

2 cups water
1 portion Pick-a-Pasta Make-Ahead Mix (see recipe, page 18)
1 to 1½ teaspoons curry powder
1 12-ounce can (1½ cups) evaporated milk
¾ cup chopped cooked chicken *or* one 5½-ounce can chunk-style chicken, cut up
1 3-ounce package cream cheese, cut up
Apple slices (optional)
Fresh mint leaves (optional)

In a 2-quart saucepan combine water, soup mix, and curry powder. Bring to boiling. Reduce heat, then simmer, covered, for 7 to 12 minutes or till pasta is tender, stirring occasionally (see photo 4, page 19). Stir in evaporated milk, chicken, and cream cheese. Increase the heat to medium-high. Cook, uncovered, for 5 to 10 minutes more or till cream cheese is melted and soup is hot, stirring occasionally. Ladle into soup bowls. Garnish each serving with apple slices and mint leaves, if desired. Makes 3 main-dish servings.

Perfect Vegetable Purees

Put your blender or food processor to work! With just a couple flicks of the switch, whirl cooked vegetables into creamy-smooth soups.

These pureed soups need no extra thickening. We've picked ingredients that will produce just the right soup consistency in these timesaving kitchen appliances.

Vichyssoise

Vichyssoise

The New York Ritz-Carlton Hotel was the first to serve the traditional vichyssoise (vish ee SWAHZ) in 1910.

3 medium potatoes (1 pound)
1 small onion, cut up
1 10¾-ounce can condensed chicken broth
1 soup can (1¼ cups) water
¼ teaspoon garlic salt
¼ teaspoon white pepper
1 cup light cream
Dairy sour cream
Watercress sprigs (optional)

Peel potatoes and cut into quarters (see photo 1). In a medium saucepan combine potatoes, onion, chicken broth, water, garlic salt, and pepper. Bring to boiling. Reduce heat, then simmer, covered, about 20 minutes or till vegetables are very tender (see photo 2).

Cool slightly, about 10 minutes. Place *half* of the mixture in a blender container or food processor bowl, then cover and blend or process for 20 to 30 seconds or till mixture is smooth (see photo 3). Pour into a mixing bowl. Repeat with remaining mixture.

Stir in the light cream (see photo 4). Cover and chill in the refrigerator for several hours or till thoroughly chilled. Ladle into soup bowls. Garnish each serving with a dollop of sour cream and watercress sprigs, if desired. Makes 5 or 6 appetizer servings.

1 Use a vegetable peeler or sharp knife to peel the potatoes. Remember to cut in a direction away from your hands. Cut out all the sprouts and green areas on the potatoes. Then quarter the peeled potatoes.

2 For a soup with a smooth consistency, cook the potatoes (and any other vegetables to be pureed) till they are *very* tender. Test them for doneness by inserting a fork. If they are done (very tender), the fork slides in and out easily.

3 Pour *half* of the mixture at a time into a blender container or food processor bowl. Blend or process it till it is very smooth. Don't blend or process the entire mixture all at once. It's too much volume and the container will overflow.

4 Stir together the second half of the pureed mixture with the first half of the pureed mixture. Then, stir in any remaining ingredients. Some pureed soups are heated before serving; others are thoroughly chilled.

Chilled Zucchini Soup

1 small potato
1 medium zucchini, peeled
1 small carrot, cut up
½ of a small onion, cut up
1½ cups chicken broth
⅛ teaspoon pepper
6 sprigs parsley
½ teaspoon Dijon-style mustard
¾ cup light cream *or* milk
1 medium tomato, seeded and chopped

Peel potato and cut into quarters (see photo 1, page 24). Coarsely chop zucchini. Stir together potato, zucchini, carrot, onion, broth, and pepper. Bring to boiling. Reduce heat. Simmer, covered, about 20 minutes or till vegetables are very tender (see photo 2, page 24).

Cool slightly, about 10 minutes. Stir in parsley and mustard. Place *half* of the mixture in a blender container or food processor bowl, then cover and blend or process for 20 to 30 seconds or till smooth (see photo 3, page 25). Pour into a bowl. Repeat with remaining mixture. Stir in cream or milk (see photo 4, page 25). Cover; chill in the refrigerator for several hours. Ladle into bowls. Garnish with tomato. Makes 4 side-dish servings.

Dilly Green Pea Soup

1 14½-ounce can chicken broth
1 10-ounce package frozen peas
2 green onions, cut up
½ teaspoon dried dillweed *or* dried mint, crushed
1 cup light cream *or* milk

In a saucepan combine broth, peas, onions, and dillweed. Bring to boiling. Reduce heat. Simmer, covered, about 15 minutes or till vegetables are very tender (see photo 2, page 24).

Cool slightly, about 10 minutes. Place *half* of the mixture in a blender container or food processor bowl, then cover and blend or process for 20 to 30 seconds or till smooth (see photo 3, page 25). Sieve, discarding pulp. Pour into a mixing bowl. Repeat with remaining mixture. Return all to the saucepan. Stir in cream or milk (see photo 4, page 25). Cook, uncovered, till heated through, stirring occasionally. Ladle into bowls. Garnish with fresh mint, if desired. Makes 3 side-dish servings.

Lentil-Pumpkin Soup

1 cup canned pumpkin *or* mashed cooked winter squash
1 small onion, cut up
2 tablespoons dry lentils
1 tablespoon instant chicken bouillon granules
⅛ teaspoon dried marjoram, crushed
⅛ teaspoon dried thyme, crushed
⅛ teaspoon pepper
Dash bottled hot pepper sauce
⅔ cup milk
Sunflower nuts

In a large saucepan combine pumpkin, onion, lentils, bouillon granules, marjoram, thyme, pepper, pepper sauce, and 2½ cups *water.* Bring to boiling. Reduce heat, then simmer, covered, for 35 to 40 minutes or till lentils and onion are very tender (see photo 2, page 24).

Cool slightly, about 10 minutes. Place *half* of the mixture in a blender container or food processor bowl, then cover and blend or process for 20 to 30 seconds or till smooth (see photo 3, page 25). Pour into a bowl. Repeat with remaining mixture. Return all to the saucepan. Stir in milk (see photo 4, page 25). Cook over low heat till heated through. Ladle into bowls. Top each serving with some of the sunflower nuts. Makes 3 side-dish servings.

Creamy Broccoli Soup

2 cups water
1 10-ounce package frozen chopped broccoli
1 medium onion, cut up
1 teaspoon instant beef bouillon granules
1 10¾-ounce can condensed cream of celery soup
½ cup dairy sour cream *or* plain yogurt
Dairy sour cream *or* plain yogurt
Ground nutmeg (optional)

In a medium saucepan combine water, broccoli, onion, and beef bouillon granules. Bring mixture to boiling. Reduce heat, then simmer, covered, about 10 minutes or till vegetables are very tender (see photo 2, page 24).

Cool slightly, about 10 minutes. Stir in soup and ½ cup sour cream or yogurt. Place *half* of the mixture in a blender container or food processor bowl, then cover and blend or process for 20 to 30 seconds or till mixture is smooth (see photo 3, page 25). Pour into a bowl. Repeat with remaining mixture. Return all to the saucepan. Cook over low heat till heated through. *Do not* boil. Ladle into bowls. Dollop with sour cream or yogurt and sprinkle with nutmeg, if desired. Makes 4 side-dish servings.

Microwave Directions: In a 2-quart microwave-safe casserole combine *½ cup* of the water, broccoli, onion, and bouillon granules. Micro-cook, covered, on 100% power (HIGH) for 8 to 10 minutes or till vegetables are very tender, stirring once (see photo 2, page 24). Cool slightly, about 10 minutes. Stir in remaining water, soup, and ½ cup sour cream or yogurt. Place *half* of the mixture in a blender container or food processor bowl, then cover and blend or process for 20 to 30 seconds or till smooth (see photo 3, page 25). Pour into a bowl. Repeat with remaining mixture. Return all to casserole. Micro-cook, uncovered, on 100% power (HIGH) for 6 to 8 minutes or till heated through, stirring twice. *Do not* boil. Ladle into bowls. Dollop with sour cream. Sprinkle with nutmeg, if desired. Makes 4 side-dish servings.

Curried Creamy Carrot Soup

1 pound carrots, thinly sliced
1 small onion, cut up
1 10¾-ounce can condensed chicken broth
1 to 1½ teaspoons curry powder
½ teaspoon dried thyme, crushed
1 clove garlic, minced
1 3-ounce package cream cheese, cut up
1 cup milk
Plain yogurt (optional)

In a large saucepan combine carrots, onion, broth, curry powder, thyme, and garlic. Bring to boiling. Reduce heat, then simmer, covered, about 20 minutes or till vegetables are very tender (see photo 2, page 24).

Cool slightly, about 10 minutes. Place *half* of the mixture and *half* of the cheese in a blender container or food processor bowl. Cover and blend or process for 20 to 30 seconds or till smooth (see photo 3, page 25). Pour into a bowl. Repeat with remaining mixture and cheese. Return all to the saucepan. Stir in milk (see photo 4, page 25). Cook, uncovered, till heated through. Ladle into soup bowls. If desired, dollop with yogurt, swirling with a spoon. Makes 4 side-dish servings.

Microwave Directions: In a 1½-quart microwave-safe casserole combine carrots, onion, *¼ cup* of the broth, curry powder, thyme, and garlic. Micro-cook, covered, on 100% power (HIGH) for 10 to 12 minutes or till vegetables are very tender, stirring twice (see photo 2, page 24). Stir in remaining broth. Cool slightly, about 10 minutes. Place *half* of the mixture and *half* of the cheese in a blender container or food processor bowl. Cover and blend or process for 20 to 30 seconds or till smooth (see photo 3, page 25). Pour into a bowl. Repeat with remaining mixture and cheese. Return all to the casserole. Stir in milk (see photo 4, page 25). Micro-cook, uncovered, on 100% power (HIGH) for 2 to 3 minutes or till hot, stirring once. Ladle into bowls. If desired, dollop with yogurt, swirling with a spoon. Makes 4 side-dish servings.

Fruit-Soup Favorites

Soup made with fruit? Serve soup for dessert?

A fruit-soup dessert sounds a bit out of the ordinary, but you're in for a pleasant surprise. The recipes in this chapter turn tasty dried fruit into perfect meal endings.

Serve them warm . . . serve them chilled. Either way, our fruit soup choices are extraordinarily delicious. Give them a try!

Apple-Cot Fruit Soup

Apple-Cot Fruit Soup

A four-way soup—serve it warm or chilled as an appetizer or for dessert.

2 inches stick cinnamon
3 whole cloves
¾ cup dried apricots
¾ cup dried apples
3 cups water
1 5½-ounce can apricot nectar
¼ cup sugar
¼ cup orange juice
1 tablespoon quick-cooking tapioca
¼ cup raisins
Orange peel twists *or* knots

For spice bag, cut a 6-inch square of several thicknesses of cheesecloth. Place stick cinnamon and whole cloves in the center of cheesecloth square. Bring sides up and tie into a bundle with string (see photo 1).

Halve large pieces of apricots and apples. In a large saucepan combine water, nectar, sugar, orange juice, tapioca, and spice bag. Let stand for 5 minutes. Add apricots, apples, and raisins. Bring to boiling. Reduce heat, then simmer, covered, for 8 to 10 minutes or till fruit is tender (see photo 2). Mixture should be slightly thickened and tapioca should be clear (see photo 3).

Remove the spice bag. Serve warm or chilled in bowls. Garnish each serving with an orange peel twist or knot (see photo 4). Makes 6 appetizer or dessert servings.

Mixed Fruit Soup

1 8-ounce package mixed dried fruit
3½ cups water
¼ cup packed brown sugar
4 teaspoons quick-cooking tapioca
¼ teaspoon ground nutmeg
1 16-ounce can pitted light sweet cherries
¼ cup orange liqueur *or* cream sherry

Pit prunes and cut fruit into bite-size pieces. In a large saucepan stir together water, brown sugar, quick-cooking tapioca, and nutmeg. Let stand for 5 minutes. Stir in dried fruit. Bring to boiling. Reduce heat, then simmer, covered, for 8 to 10 minutes or till fruit is tender (see photo 2). Mixture should be slightly thickened and tapioca should be clear (see photo 3).

Stir in *undrained* cherries and orange liqueur or sherry. Heat through. Serve warm or chilled in bowls. Makes 8 appetizer or dessert servings.

1 To make a spice bag, cut three 6-inch squares of clean cheesecloth for cooking. Stack the squares on top of each other and place the spices in the center. Bring the edges of the cheesecloth together and tie them securely with a string. Having all the spices in a cheesecloth bag makes them easy to remove from the hot soup.

2 Near the end of the simmering time, test the dried fruit for doneness. Use a fork to pierce a piece of the dried fruit. When it's done, the fork will slide in and out of the fruit very easily.

3 At the end of the simmering time, the tapioca should be clear (see spoon on the right). If it's not yet clear (see spoon on the left), allow the soup to simmer for a few minutes more.

4 To make an orange peel garnish, use a vegetable peeler to cut long, wide strips of peel from the orange. Place the wide strips on a cutting board and use a sharp knife to cut it into long strips about ¼ inch wide. Curl the narrow strips around your finger to make an orange peel twist. Or, tie the strips of peel into a loose knot for an orange peel knot.

Take Stock

You don't have to speculate in the stock market to enjoy these five outstanding soup stocks.

Our stocks produce delicious dividends, yet require minimal investment in pot watching and ingredients. Enjoy them as is . . . or use as a base for other savory soups found throughout this book.

Want a hot tip? We also tell you what soup stocks to choose when you're short on time.

Beef Stock

Beef Stock

With a splash of sherry, a few fresh mushrooms, and a little sliced green onion, you can transform this ordinary stock into an elegant appetizer soup.

4 pounds meaty beef soup bones (beef shank crosscuts, short ribs, knuckle, *or* marrow bones)
2 medium yellow onions
3 carrots, cut up
8 sprigs parsley
10 whole black peppercorns
4 bay leaves
4 cloves garlic, halved
1 tablespoon dried basil, crushed
1½ teaspoons salt
10 cups water

Place meat bones in a large shallow roasting pan, then bake, uncovered, in a 450° oven about 30 minutes or till bones are well browned, turning once or twice. Drain off fat. For stock, place meat bones in a 6- or 8-quart Dutch oven or stockpot.

Cut onions into wedges (see photo 1). Add onions, carrots, parsley, peppercorns, bay leaves, garlic, basil, and salt to browned bones (see photo 2). Add water. Bring to boiling. Reduce heat, then simmer, covered, for 3½ hours. Remove meat bones; set aside.

To strain, pour stock through a large colander or sieve lined with 2 layers of cheesecloth (see photo 3). Discard vegetables and seasonings. Clarify stock, if desired (see tip, page 37).

Remove fat (see photos 4 and 5). If desired, when bones are cool enough to handle, remove meat from bones and reserve meat for another use. Discard bones. Store stock and reserved meat in separate covered containers in the refrigerator for up to 3 days or in the freezer for up to 6 months. Label type of stock, the quantity, and date. Makes about 8 cups stock.

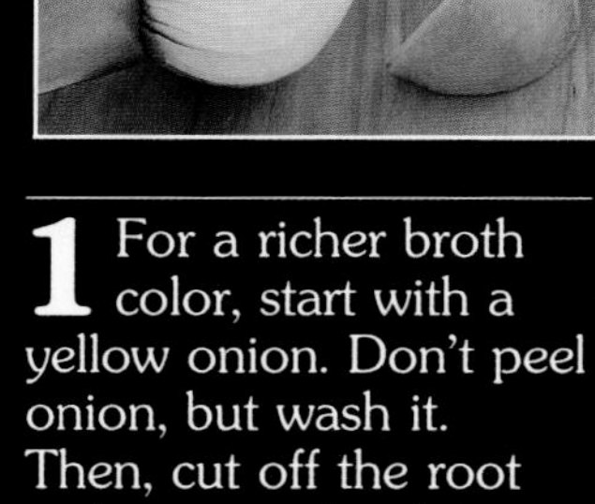

1 For a richer broth color, start with a yellow onion. Don't peel onion, but wash it. Then, cut off the root and stem ends of the onion. Cut the onion into wedges.

2 Sprinkle the crushed basil over the carrots, onion wedges, parsley, peppercorns, garlic, and bay leaves. Be sure to use a 6- or 8-quart Dutch oven or stockpot so it will be large enough to hold all the ingredients.

3 To strain the stock, line a large colander or sieve with two layers of clean cheesecloth for cooking. Set it in a large heat-proof bowl or container. Ladle or pour stock through the lined colander. Discard vegetables and seasonings.

4 One way of removing the fat from the hot stock is to use a large metal spoon and skim off the fat that rises to the top.

5 Another way of removing the fat is to chill the stock in the refrigerator for 6 to 8 hours. Then use a spoon to lift off the fat that solidifies on the surface of the stock.

Chicken Stock

3½ pounds bony chicken pieces (backs, necks, and wings from 3 chickens)
2 medium yellow onions
3 stalks celery with leaves, cut up
4 whole cloves
1 tablespoon dried oregano, crushed
8 cups water

For stock, place chicken pieces in a 6- or 8-quart Dutch oven or stockpot. Cut onions into wedges (see photo 1, page 34). Add onions, celery, cloves, oregano, 1 teaspoon *salt*, and ½ teaspoon *pepper* to chicken pieces (see photo 2, page 34). Add water. Bring to boiling. Reduce heat, then simmer, covered, for 2 hours. Lift out chicken pieces with a slotted spoon; set aside.

To strain, pour stock through a colander or sieve lined with 2 layers of cheesecloth (see photo 3, page 34). Discard vegetables and seasonings. Clarify stock, if desired (see tip, opposite).

Remove fat (see photos 4 and 5, page 35). If desired, when bones are cool enough to handle, remove meat from bones and reserve meat for another use. Discard bones. Store stock and reserved meat in separate covered containers in the refrigerator for up to 3 days or in the freezer for up to 6 months. Label type of stock, the quantity, and date. Makes about 7 cups stock.

Fish Stock

3 pounds fresh *or* frozen fish heads and tails *or* drawn lean fish (cod, pike, flounder, haddock, hake, orange roughy, *or* porgy)
1 medium yellow onion
¼ cup lemon juice
2 stalks celery with leaves, cut up
3 cloves garlic, halved
1 tablespoon grated gingerroot *or* 1 teaspoon ground ginger
1 tablespoon dried marjoram, crushed
½ teaspoon dry mustard

Thaw fish, if frozen; rinse. Place fish in a 6-quart Dutch oven or stockpot. Cut onion into wedges (see photo 1, page 34). Add onion, lemon juice, celery, garlic, gingerroot or ginger, marjoram, mustard, and ½ teaspoon *salt* to fish (see photo 2, page 34). Add 8 cups *water*. Bring to boiling. Reduce heat. Simmer, covered, for 1 hour.

To strain, pour stock through colander or sieve lined with 2 layers of cheesecloth (see photo 3, page 34). Discard fish, vegetables, and seasonings. Clarify stock, if desired (see tip, opposite).

Store stock in a covered container in the refrigerator for up to 2 days or in the freezer for up to 6 months. Label type of stock, the quantity, and date. Makes about 6 cups stock.

Stock Options

When you're in a hurry and don't have time to make homemade stock from scratch, you need to know your options.

For the recipes in this book, you can use one of the homemade stock recipes from this chapter or one of the convenient commercial substitutes. Instant bouillon granules or cubes come in beef, chicken, and vegetable flavors. Just mix these with water, according to the package directions, before using them as broth.

You can buy ready-to-use canned broth. The cans usually contain 14½ ounces, which is about 1¾ cups of broth. If you choose to use canned *condensed* chicken or beef broth, before using it, dilute it with water according to the can directions.

Veal Stock

4 pounds veal knuckle, cut up
2 medium yellow onions
2 cups mushrooms, cut up
3 leeks, cut up
10 whole black peppercorns
2 bay leaves
1 teaspoon fennel seed
2 cups dry white wine

For stock, place veal in a 6- or 8-quart Dutch oven or stockpot. Cut onions into wedges (see photo 1, page 34). Add onions, mushrooms, leeks, peppercorns, bay leaves, fennel, and ½ teaspoon *salt* to veal (see photo 2, page 34). Add wine and 6 cups *water*. Bring to boiling. Reduce heat. Simmer, covered, for 2 hours. Lift out meat bones with a slotted spoon; set aside.

To strain, pour stock through a large colander or sieve lined with 2 layers of cheesecloth (see photo 3, page 34). Discard vegetables and seasonings. Clarify stock, if desired (see tip, below).

Remove fat (see photos 4 and 5, page 35). If desired, when bones are cool, remove meat and reserve for another use. Discard bones. Store stock and meat in separate covered containers in the refrigerator for up to 3 days or in the freezer for up to 6 months. Label type of stock, quantity, and date. Makes about 6 cups stock.

Vegetable Stock

4 medium yellow onions
4 medium carrots, cut up
3 medium potatoes, cut up
2 parsnips *or* turnips, cut up
1 small head cabbage, cut up
¼ cup butter *or* margarine
1 teaspoon dried dillweed

Scrub all vegetables, remove root and stem ends. *Do not* peel vegetables, unless coated with wax. Cut onions into wedges (see photo 1, page 34). In a 6-quart Dutch oven or stockpot melt butter or margarine. For stock, add onions, carrots, potatoes, parsnips or turnips, cabbage, dillweed, 1 teaspoon *salt,* and ¼ teaspoon *pepper* to butter or margarine (see photo 2, page 34). Cover and cook over low heat about 30 minutes or till vegetables are tender, stirring occasionally. Add 8 cups *water.* Bring mixture to boiling. Reduce heat. Simmer, covered, for 2 hours.

To strain, pour the stock through a large colander or sieve lined with 2 layers of cheesecloth (see photo 3, page 34). Discard the vegetables and seasonings.

Store stock in a covered container in the refrigerator for up to 3 days or in the freezer for up to 6 months. Label type of stock, the quantity, and date. Makes about 6½ cups stock.

Clarifying Stock

For a clear stock, separate an *egg,* reserving the shell. Crush the shell. Save the yolk for another use. In a Dutch oven stir together the strained broth, ¼ cup *cold water,* egg white, and shell. Bring to boiling. Remove from the heat and let stand for 5 minutes. Strain the stock again through a large colander or sieve lined with several layers of damp cheesecloth.

Vegetable-Packed Soups

"Eat your vegetables, they're good for you." That's healthy advice, but sometimes it's hard to follow.

We make it simple to do and delicious, too. Just serve a steaming bowl of soup—one that's chock-full of vegetables. It's so-o-o satisfying.

Minestrone

Minestrone

1 medium potato, peeled
1 carrot
6 cups Beef Stock (see recipe, page 34), Vegetable Stock (see recipe, page 37), *or* beef broth (see tip, page 36)
1 15-ounce can great northern beans
1 14-ounce can peeled Italian-style tomatoes, cut up
1 cup shredded cabbage
1 medium onion, chopped (½ cup)
2 cloves garlic, minced
¾ teaspoon dried chervil *or* basil, crushed
¾ teaspoon dried oregano, crushed
¼ teaspoon pepper
2 ounces thin spaghetti
1 small zucchini, halved lengthwise and sliced
1 9-ounce package frozen Italian green beans *or* cut green beans
Grated Parmesan cheese

Cut potato into julienne strips (see photo 1). Bias-slice carrot ¼ inch thick (see photo 2).

In a Dutch oven combine potato; carrot; Beef Stock, Vegetable Stock, or beef broth; *undrained* northern beans; *undrained* tomatoes; cabbage; onion; garlic; chervil or basil; oregano; and pepper. Bring to boiling (see photo 3).

Break long spaghetti pieces into fourths. Stir spaghetti, zucchini, and green beans into vegetable mixture in Dutch oven. Return to boiling. Reduce heat, then simmer, covered, for 5 to 10 minutes or till vegetables and pasta are done (see photo 4).

Season to taste with salt. Ladle into soup bowls. Sprinkle each serving with Parmesan cheese. Makes 8 side-dish servings.

1 To make julienne vegetable strips, cut peeled vegetables (such as potatoes or carrots) into pieces that are the length you desire. Then, slice vegetable lengthwise about ⅛ to ¼ inch thick. Stack 2 or 3 of the slices and make lengthwise cuts ⅛ to ¼ wide, forming matchsticklike strips.

2 For bias-sliced vegetables, make the first cut diagonally across the end of the vegetable. Then, follow through with the remaining cuts at the same angle, as shown. Slice the vegetable into even widths.

3 After ingredients are added, quickly bring the mixture to boiling over high heat. The mixture is boiling when the bubbles rise to the surface and break.

4 Turn the heat down after the soup comes to a boil. Adjust the heat to maintain a simmer—a few bubbles form slowly and burst before they reach the surface. Then, cover the Dutch oven.

Borscht

When time is short, make the speedy version using canned beets and frozen spinach.

2 pounds medium beets with tops
3 medium turnips (about 1¼ pounds)
2 stalks celery
5 cups Beef Stock (see recipe, page 34) *or* beef broth (see tip, page 36)
2 medium carrots, shredded (1 cup)
1 large onion, chopped (1 cup)
2 cloves garlic, minced
½ of a 6-ounce can tomato paste
2 tablespoons vinegar
1 tablespoon sugar
1 teaspoon salt
1 teaspoon dried marjoram, crushed
¼ teaspoon pepper
½ cup dairy sour cream

Wash beets and turnips; peel. Reserve beet tops. If beet tops are fresh-looking, crisp, and reasonably unblemished, thoroughly wash in cool water to remove dirt and sand particles. Remove damaged portions, then finely chop. (*Or,* substitute 2 cups finely chopped spinach for the beet tops.) Cut beets and turnips into julienne strips (see photo 1, page 40). Bias-slice celery ½ inch thick (see photo 2, page 41).

In a Dutch oven combine beets and tops (or spinach), turnips, celery, Beef Stock or beef broth, carrots, onion, and garlic. Stir in tomato paste, vinegar, sugar, salt, marjoram, and pepper. Bring to boiling (see photo 3, page 41). Reduce heat, then simmer, covered, about 30 minutes or till vegetables are tender (see photo 4, page 41). Ladle into soup bowls. Dollop each serving with sour cream. If desired, serve with dark rye bread. Makes 8 side-dish servings.

Speedy Borscht: Prepare Borscht as above, *except* substitute three 16-ounce cans *julienne beets* for fresh beets and turnips and one 10-ounce package frozen chopped *spinach* for beet tops. Continue as directed, adding drained canned beets and frozen spinach the last 10 minutes of cooking.

Hot and Sour Parsnip Soup

Oriental chefs serve a similar soup with the same delicate strands of cooked egg. To get those thin ribbons, follow this tip from our Test Kitchen: Add the egg and then stir gently.

2 small parsnips (about 4 ounces)
4 cups Chicken Stock (see recipe, page 36) *or* chicken broth (see tip, page 36)
1 cup mushrooms, thinly sliced
½ cup chopped water chestnuts
3 tablespoons rice wine vinegar *or* white vinegar
2 tablespoons dry sherry
2 tablespoons soy sauce
1 tablespoon grated gingerroot
½ teaspoon pepper
2 green onions
2 cups diced tofu (fresh bean curd)
1 beaten egg

Scrape or peel parsnips to remove outer skin. Cut parsnips into julienne strips (see photo 1, page 40).

In a large saucepan or Dutch oven combine parsnip strips, Chicken Stock or chicken broth, mushrooms, water chestnuts, rice wine vinegar or white vinegar, dry sherry, soy sauce, gingerroot, and pepper. Bring to boiling (see photo 3, page 41). Reduce heat, then simmer, covered, for 10 to 15 minutes or till parsnips are tender (see photo 4, page 41).

Bias-slice green onions ¼ inch wide (see photo 2, page 41). Stir green onions and tofu into vegetable mixture in the saucepan. Simmer, covered, for 2 to 3 minutes. Pour egg slowly *(do not stir)* into hot soup in a thin stream, then stir gently 2 or 3 times till egg cooks and shreds finely. Ladle into soup bowls. Makes 3 or 4 main-dish servings.

Carrot-Barley Chowder

- **6 small carrots**
- **2 stalks celery**
- **4 cups Chicken Stock (see recipe, page 36) *or* chicken broth (see tip, page 36)**
- **3 medium leeks, thinly sliced (2 cups)**
- **2 medium potatoes, peeled and chopped (2 cups)**
- **½ cup quick-cooking barley**
- **½ teaspoon salt**
- **½ teaspoon ground nutmeg**
- **¼ teaspoon pepper**
- **2 cups light cream**
- **Snipped parsley (optional)**

Cut carrot into julienne strips (see photo 1, page 40). Bias-slice celery ½ inch thick (see photo 2, page 41).

In a large saucepan or Dutch oven combine carrots, celery, Chicken Stock or chicken broth, leeks, potatoes, barley, salt, nutmeg, and pepper. Bring to boiling (see photo 3, page 41). Reduce heat, then simmer, covered, about 15 minutes or till vegetables are tender (see photo 4, page 41).

Stir in cream. Heat through. Season to taste with salt and pepper. Ladle into soup bowls. Sprinkle each serving with snipped parsley, if desired. Makes 6 to 8 side-dish servings.

Spicy Split Pea Soup

- **1 pound dry yellow *or* green split peas**
- **6 cups Chicken Stock (see recipe, page 36) *or* chicken broth (see tip, page 36)**
- **1 large onion, chopped (1 cup)**
- **2 cloves garlic, minced**
- **1 teaspoon ground cumin**
- **½ teaspoon ground mace**
- **½ teaspoon paprika**
- **½ teaspoon ground red pepper**
- **½ teaspoon ground cinnamon**
- **2 medium carrots**
- **1 16-ounce can tomatoes, cut up**
- **1 medium green pepper, chopped (¾ cup)**
- **1 cup hot cooked rice *or* ½ cup chopped peanuts**

Place peas in a colander; rinse. In a Dutch oven combine peas, Chicken Stock or broth, onion, garlic, cumin, mace, paprika, red pepper, cinnamon, and ½ teaspoon *salt*. Bring to boiling (see photo 3, page 41). Reduce heat, then simmer, covered, about 1 hour or till peas are tender (see photo 4, page 41). Mash peas slightly.

Bias-slice carrots ¼ inch thick (see photo 2, page 41). Add carrots, *undrained* tomatoes, and green pepper to broth mixture. Bring to boiling. Reduce heat, then simmer, covered, 10 to 15 minutes or till carrots are tender. Ladle into soup bowls. Top with a small mound of rice or peanuts. Makes 6 main-dish servings.

Presto! It's Pesto!

Pesto, long enjoyed on pasta, is a tasty addition to any homemade soup.

To make Basil Pesto, place ½ cup firmly packed snipped fresh *basil;* ½ small *carrot,* grated; ¼ cup lightly packed *parsley;* ¼ cup grated *Parmesan or Romano cheese;* 2 tablespoons chopped *walnuts;* 1 clove *garlic;* and ⅛ teaspoon *salt* in a blender container or food processor bowl. Cover and blend or process with several on/off turns till a paste forms. With machine running, gradually add 3 tablespoons *cooking oil;* blend or process till the consistency of soft butter. Makes ½ cup.

Fisherman's Catch

Where are the fish biting? It doesn't matter—skip the fishing trip! Instead, cast off for the nearest neighborhood supermarket.

Bring home your prized "catch" of the day and simmer it in a sumptuous soup. Then, be ready to reel in the compliments. These soups will win your family's approval . . . hook, line, and sinker!

Seafood Chowder

Seafood Chowder

- **12 ounces fresh *or* frozen fish fillets (cod, pike, *or* orange roughy)**
- **8 ounces fresh *or* frozen shelled shrimp**
- **2 cups Fish Stock (see recipe, page 36) *or* chicken broth (see tip, page 36)**
- **1 cup sliced fresh mushrooms**
- **1 large carrot, sliced (¾ cup)**
- **1 medium onion, chopped (½ cup)**
- **1 clove garlic, minced**
- **½ teaspoon dried marjoram, crushed**
- **⅛ teaspoon salt**
- **⅛ teaspoon pepper**
- **1 bay leaf**
- **1 15-ounce can tomato sauce**
- **2 large tomatoes, peeled, seeded, and chopped**
- **2 tablespoons snipped parsley**
- **½ teaspoon finely shredded lemon peel**

Thaw fish and shrimp, if frozen. Remove skin from fish, if present. Cut fish into 1-inch pieces (see photo 1). Devein shrimp. Chill fish and shrimp in the refrigerator till ready to use.

In a large saucepan combine Fish Stock or chicken broth, mushrooms, carrot, onion, garlic, marjoram, salt, pepper, and bay leaf. Bring to boiling. Reduce heat, then simmer, covered, for 10 minutes or till vegetables are tender.

Stir in tomato sauce and tomatoes. Add fish and shrimp (see photo 2). Bring just to boiling. Reduce heat, then simmer, covered, for 2 to 3 minutes or till shrimp are done and fish flakes easily with a fork (see photo 3). Stir once. Discard bay leaf. Season soup to taste with salt.

In a small bowl combine parsley and lemon peel. Ladle into soup bowls and sprinkle parsley mixture atop. Serve with French bread, if desired. Makes 4 main-dish servings.

1 Cut the thawed fish into pieces with a sharp knife. For even cooking, make the pieces as uniform in size and shape as possible. Place fish pieces in a bowl, then cover and chill till needed.

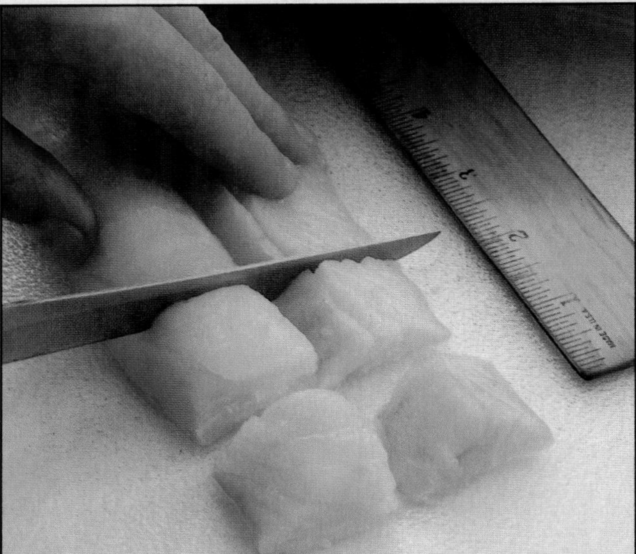

2 Carefully spoon fish and shrimp into the hot chowder so that it doesn't splash or break apart. Add fish at the specified time to keep it from overcooking.

3 To test the fish for doneness, remove a piece of fish and insert a fork. The flesh flakes easily and the fish has an opaque appearance when it's properly cooked.

Fish-Succotash Chowder

Neufchâtel cheese melts right into the soup, making it so-o-o creamy!

12 ounces fresh *or* frozen fish fillets (red snapper *or* sole)
3 cups Chicken Stock (see recipe, page 36), Fish Stock (see recipe, page 36), *or* chicken broth (see tip, page 36)
1 10-ounce package frozen succotash
1 stalk celery, sliced (½ cup)
1 medium onion, chopped (½ cup)
¼ cup long grain rice
½ teaspoon dried dillweed
¼ teaspoon lemon pepper
1 8-ounce package Neufchâtel cheese, cut into cubes
Fresh dill (optional)

Thaw fish, if frozen. Remove skin from fish, if present. Cut fish into 1-inch pieces (see photo 1, page 46). Chill fish in the refrigerator till ready to use.

In a large saucepan combine 2 *cups* of the Chicken Stock or Fish Stock or chicken broth, succotash, celery, onion, *uncooked* rice, dillweed, and lemon pepper. Bring to boiling. Reduce heat, then simmer, covered, about 15 minutes or till vegetables and rice are tender.

Add cheese and remaining stock or broth. Heat and stir till cheese is melted. Add fish (see photo 2, page 47). Bring just to boiling. Reduce heat, then simmer, covered, for 2 to 3 minutes or till fish flakes easily with a fork (see photo 3, page 47). Stir once. Ladle into soup bowls. Garnish with a sprig of fresh dill, if desired. Makes 4 main-dish servings.

Cream of Artichoke And Fish Chowder

12 ounces fresh *or* frozen fish fillets, (cod, haddock, *or* sole)
2½ cups Fish Stock (see recipe, page 36) *or* chicken broth (see tip, page 36)
1 10-ounce package frozen artichoke hearts
1 medium carrot, chopped (½ cup)
1 stalk celery, sliced (½ cup)
1 medium onion, chopped (½ cup)
½ teaspoon dried oregano, crushed
¼ teaspoon salt
¼ teaspoon dried thyme, crushed
⅛ teaspoon ground red pepper
1 cup whipping cream
½ cup sliced fresh mushrooms

Thaw fish, if frozen. Remove skin from fish, if present. Cut fish into 1-inch pieces (see photo 1, page 46). Chill fish in the refrigerator till ready to use.

In a large saucepan combine Fish Stock or chicken broth, artichokes, carrot, celery, onion, oregano, salt, thyme, and pepper. Bring to boiling. Reduce heat, then simmer, covered, about 10 minutes or till vegetables are tender.

Add fish (see photo 2, page 47). Bring just to boiling. Reduce heat, then simmer, covered, for 2 to 3 minutes or till fish flakes easily with a fork (see photo 3, page 47). Stir once. Stir in the whipping cream and sliced mushrooms. Heat through but *do not boil.* Ladle into soup bowls. Makes 4 main-dish servings.

Fish and Spinach Chowder

12 ounces fresh *or* frozen fish fillets (lake perch, pike, *or* orange roughy)
2 cups Chicken Stock (see recipe, page 36) *or* chicken broth (see tip, page 36)
1 cup finely chopped fresh spinach
1 large potato, peeled and diced (about 1 cup)
1 small onion, finely chopped (¼ cup)
2 cloves garlic, minced
2½ cups milk
½ teaspoon salt
Dash bottled hot pepper sauce
¼ cup grated Romano *or* Parmesan cheese

Thaw fish, if frozen. Remove skin from fish, if present. Cut fish into 1-inch pieces (see photo 1, page 46). Chill fish in the refrigerator till ready to use.

In a large saucepan combine Chicken Stock or broth, spinach, potato, onion, and garlic. Bring to boiling. Reduce heat, then simmer, covered, for 5 to 10 minutes or till potato is tender.

Stir in milk, salt, and hot pepper sauce. Add fish (see photo 2, page 47). Bring just to boiling. Reduce heat, then simmer, covered, for 2 to 3 minutes or till fish flakes easily with a fork (see photo 3, page 47). Stir once. Ladle into soup bowls. Sprinkle each serving with grated cheese. Makes 4 main-dish servings.

Fish and Rice Soup

1 pound fresh *or* frozen fish fillets (cod, pike, *or* haddock)
3 cups Chicken Stock (see recipe, page 36) *or* chicken broth (see tip, page 36)
1 15-ounce can tomato sauce
1 medium green pepper, chopped (¾ cup)
½ cup long grain rice
¼ cup dry red wine
½ teaspoon dried savory, crushed
Dash garlic powder
Several dashes bottled hot pepper sauce

Thaw fish, if frozen. Remove skin from fish, if present. Cut fish into 1-inch pieces (see photo 1, page 46). Chill fish in the refrigerator till ready to use.

In a large saucepan combine Chicken Stock or chicken broth, tomato sauce, green pepper, *uncooked* rice, wine, savory, garlic powder, and hot pepper sauce. Bring to boiling. Reduce heat, then simmer, covered, for 15 to 20 minutes or till rice is done.

Add fish (see photo 2, page 47). Bring just to boiling. Reduce heat, then simmer, covered, for 2 to 3 minutes or till fish flakes easily with a fork (see photo 3, page 47). Stir once. Ladle into soup bowls. Makes 4 main-dish servings.

Tortilla Soup Bowls

Looking for a way to wow your guests or family? Serve them a creamy soup or hearty stew in uniquely shaped bowls made from tortillas. They're easy to create.

To make the "bowls," in a large skillet warm 9- or 10-inch flour tortillas over low heat just till warm and pliable. Place each warm tortilla into an ovenproof soup bowl, fluting the tortilla as necessary to fit the bowl. Place the soup bowls containing the tortillas on a baking sheet. Bake in a 350° oven about 10 minutes. To serve, ladle soup or stew into the tortilla "bowls" placed in soup bowls.

Soups Made With Meat

Don't shortchange family meals just because you're watching your pennies.

How can you carry out this frugal feat? Simply simmer less expensive meat cuts in a richly seasoned broth. These wise meat buys turn out hearty soups loaded with flavor.

Beefy Vegetable Soup

Beefy Vegetable Soup

2 pounds meaty beef short ribs *or* beef shank crosscuts
6 cups water
1 large onion, chopped (1 cup)
1½ teaspoons salt
¼ teaspoon pepper
Bouquet Garni
2 cups cubed butternut squash (about 10 ounces)
1 15½-ounce can red kidney beans, drained
1 12-ounce can whole kernel corn with sweet peppers, drained
1 6-ounce package frozen pea pods, halved diagonally

Select either the beef short ribs or crosscuts and trim off excess fat (see photo 1).

In a Dutch oven combine meat, water, onion, salt, and pepper. Prepare Bouquet Garni (see photo 2). Add to Dutch oven. Bring to boiling. Reduce heat, then simmer, covered, for 1½ to 2 hours or till meat is tender (see photo 3).

Remove meat from soup; set aside. Skim fat from soup (see photos 4 and 5, page 35). Add squash to soup. Bring to boiling. Reduce heat, then simmer, covered, about 10 minutes or till squash is done.

Meanwhile, when meat is cool enough to handle, remove meat from bones. Cut up meat (see photo 4). Discard bones. Return meat to soup along with beans and corn (see photo 5). Bring to boiling. Add pea pods. Reduce heat, then simmer, covered, for 1 to 2 minutes or till peas are done. Remove Bouquet Garni. Ladle into soup bowls. Makes 6 main-dish servings.

Bouquet Garni: Place 4 sprigs *parsley;* leaves from 3 *stalks celery; 2 bay leaves;* 2 cloves *garlic,* halved; and 2 tablespoons snipped fresh *thyme or* 2 teaspoons *dried thyme* on a double thickness of cheesecloth. Tie into a bag.

1 Select either beef short ribs (front) or beef shank crosscuts (back) when making soup. Trim as much fat as possible before adding meat to the soup and you'll end with a fat-trimmed broth.

2 To tie up seasonings, use a double thickness of clean cheesecloth for cooking. Trim excess cloth after tying. This classic method of adding seasonings simplifies removal after cooking.

3 To check meat for doneness after simmering, pierce a meaty piece with a fork. The fork should insert and slip out easily.

4 Prevent burned fingers by letting the meat cool slightly before cutting it into small pieces.

5 Add canned and precooked vegetables and meat near the end of cooking. They only need a few minutes to heat through.

Carbonnade-Style Beef Soup

Both acini de pepe and rosamarina are small pasta—perfect for soup making. Acini de pepe looks like little peppercorns and the rosamarina is ricelike.

- **1½ pounds meaty beef short ribs *or* beef shank crosscuts**
- **3 cups water**
- **1 12-ounce can beer (1½ cups)**
- **½ medium rutabaga, chopped (about 1 cup)**
- **1 medium potato, chopped (about ½ cup)**
- **1 1- or 1¼-ounce envelope *regular* onion-mushroom soup mix**
- **¾ teaspoon dried marjoram, crushed**
- **¼ cup acini de pepe *or* rosamarina pasta (2 ounces)**

Select either the beef short ribs or crosscuts and trim off excess fat (see photo 1, page 52).

In a Dutch oven or large saucepan combine meat, water, and beer. Bring to boiling. Reduce heat, then simmer, covered, for 1½ to 2 hours or till meat is tender (see photo 3, page 53).

Remove meat from soup; set aside. Skim fat from soup (see photos 4 and 5, page 35). When meat is cool enough to handle, remove meat from bones. Cut up meat (see photo 4, page 53). Discard bones.

Return meat to soup along with rutabaga, potato, soup mix, and marjoram (see photo 5, page 53). Bring to boiling. Reduce heat, then simmer, covered, 15 minutes. Add pasta. Cover and simmer about 10 minutes more or till pasta is tender. Ladle into soup bowls. Makes 3 main-dish servings.

Ham and Rice Soup

- **4 smoked pork hocks (about 1½ pounds)**
- **5 cups water**
- **1 stalk celery, sliced (½ cup)**
- **1½ teaspoons dried oregano, crushed**
- **2 bay leaves**
- **1 clove garlic, minced**
- **½ teaspoon seasoned salt**
- **¼ teaspoon pepper**
- **2 small zucchini, halved lengthwise and sliced ½ inch thick**
- **⅓ cup long grain rice**

In a Dutch oven combine meat, water, celery, oregano, bay leaves, garlic, seasoned salt, and pepper. Bring to boiling. Reduce heat, then simmer, covered, for 1½ to 2 hours or till meat is tender (see photo 3, page 53).

Remove meat from soup; set aside. Remove and discard bay leaves. Skim fat from soup (see photos 4 and 5, page 35). When meat is cool enough to handle, remove meat from bones. Cut up meat (see photo 4, page 53). Discard bones.

Return meat to soup along with zucchini and *uncooked* rice. Bring to boiling. Reduce heat, then simmer, covered, for 15 to 20 minutes or till rice is tender. Ladle into soup bowls. Makes 4 main-dish servings.

Keep Soup Hot or Keep It Cold

Serve soup at just the right temperature by heating or chilling the individual bowls or mugs. Run the containers under hot tap water to heat them. Or, chill them in the refrigerator for icy cold soups.

Short Rib-Sauerkraut Soup

- **1 pound meaty beef short ribs**
- **4 cups water**
- **½ teaspoon salt**
- **¼ teaspoon pepper**
- **1 clove garlic, minced**
- **1 16-ounce can sauerkraut**
- **1 large potato, chopped (1 cup)**
- **½ of a 12-ounce package fully cooked smoked sausage links, cut into ½-inch slices**
- **1 medium onion, chopped (½ cup)**
- **1 teaspoon dried dillweed**
- **¼ teaspoon caraway seed**
- **Dairy Sour Cream (optional)**

Trim off excess fat from meat (see photo 1, page 52). In a Dutch oven combine meat, water, salt, pepper, and garlic. Bring to boiling. Reduce heat, then simmer, covered, for 1½ to 2 hours or till meat is tender (see photo 3, page 53).

Remove meat from soup; set aside. Skim fat from soup (see photos 4 and 5, page 35). When meat is cool enough to handle, remove meat from bones. Cut up meat (see photo 4, page 53). Discard bones.

Return meat to soup along with *undrained* sauerkraut, potato, sausage, onion, dillweed, and caraway seed. Bring to boiling. Reduce heat, then simmer, covered, 15 minutes or till potatoes are tender. Ladle into soup bowls. Dollop each serving with sour cream, if desired. Makes 4 main-dish servings.

Beef and Lentil Soup

Lentils boost the protein.

- **1 pound beef shank crosscuts**
- **4 cups water**
- **2 cups tomato juice**
- **1 medium onion, chopped (½ cup)**
- **1 teaspoon salt**
- **¼ teaspoon pepper**
- **8 ounces dry lentils (about 1 cup)**
- **1 16-ounce can tomatoes, cut up**
- **1 teaspoon dried thyme, crushed**
- **2 tablespoons snipped parsley**

Trim off excess fat from meat (see photo 1, page 52). In a Dutch oven combine meat, water, tomato juice, onion, salt, and pepper. Bring to boiling. Reduce heat, then simmer, covered, for 45 minutes.

Meanwhile, rinse lentils. Add lentils, *undrained* tomatoes, and thyme to Dutch oven. Bring to boiling. Reduce heat, then simmer, covered, for 45 minutes more or till lentils are done and meat is tender (see photo 3, page 53).

Remove meat from soup; set aside. Skim fat from soup (see photos 4 and 5, page 35). When meat is cool enough to handle, remove meat from bones. Cut up meat (see photo 4, page 53). Discard bones.

Return meat to soup and heat through. Sprinkle with parsley. Ladle into soup bowls. Makes 6 main-dish servings.

Barley-Beef Soup

- **2 pounds beef shank crosscuts**
- **6 cups water**
- **1 large onion, chopped (1 cup)**
- **¾ cup dry red wine**
- **1½ teaspoons salt**
- **1 teaspoon finely shredded orange peel**
- **¼ teaspoon pepper**
- **1 clove garlic, minced**
- **¾ cup quick-cooking barley**
- **1 medium green pepper, chopped (¾ cup)**

Trim off excess fat from meat (see photo 1, page 52). In a Dutch oven combine meat, water, onion, wine, salt, orange peel, pepper, and garlic. Bring to boiling. Reduce heat, then simmer, covered, for 1½ to 2 hours or till meat is tender (see photo 3, page 53).

Remove meat from soup; set aside. Skim fat from soup (see photos 4 and 5, page 35). When meat is cool enough to handle, remove meat from bones. Cut up meat (see photo 4, page 53). Discard bones.

Return meat to soup along with *uncooked* barley and green pepper. Bring to boiling. Reduce heat, then simmer, covered, about 10 minutes or till barley and pepper are tender. Ladle into soup bowls. Makes 4 main-dish servings.

◀ *Lamb-Sausage Soup*

Lamb-Sausage Soup

Spinach Pesto adds a powerfully good flavor punch.

- **2 meaty lamb shanks (about 1½ pounds)**
- **6 cups water**
- **1 medium onion, chopped (½ cup)**
- **¼ teaspoon pepper**
- **8 ounces Polish sausage, cut into ½-inch slices**
- **1 10-ounce package frozen whole kernel corn**
- **1 cup frozen crinkle-cut carrots**
- **1 7½-ounce can tomatoes, cut up**
- **1 medium zucchini, halved lengthwise and sliced ¼ inch thick (1 cup)**
- **Spinach Pesto**

Trim off excess fat from meat (see photo 1, page 52). In a Dutch oven combine meat, water, onion, and pepper. Bring to boiling. Reduce heat, then simmer, covered, for 2 hours or till meat is tender (see photo 3, page 53).

Remove meat from soup; set aside. Skim fat from soup (see photos 4 and 5, page 35). When meat is cool enough to handle, remove meat from bones. Cut up meat (see photo 4, page 53). Discard bones.

Return meat to soup along with sausage, corn, carrots, and *undrained* tomatoes. Bring to boiling. Reduce heat, then simmer, covered, for 5 minutes. Add zucchini. Simmer, covered, about 5 minutes more or till vegetables are tender. Ladle into soup bowls. Top each with a dollop of Spinach Pesto. Makes 5 main-dish servings.

Spinach Pesto: Place ½ cup firmly packed fresh *spinach,* ¼ cup lightly packed *parsley,* ¼ cup grated *Parmesan cheese,* 2 tablespoons *almonds,* and 1 clove *garlic* in a blender container or food processor bowl. Cover and blend or process with several on/off turns till a paste forms. With machine running, gradually add 3 tablespoons *cooking oil;* blend or process till the consistency of soft butter. Makes ½ cup.

Oyster and Clam Specialties

A tantalizing adventure awaits you! When you open oyster and clam shells, it's like opening the door to a sensational seafood treasure.

Put that treasure to good use. Just cook the plump oysters to make a scrumptious stew. Or, simmer the clams in a mouth-watering chowder.

Dig into a savory bowlful. You're in for a tip-top taste experience.

Elegant Oyster Stew

Elegant Oyster Stew

Substitute 1 pint shucked small oysters or two 8-ounce cans whole oysters for the live oysters in the shell.

24 oysters, chilled
3 slices bacon, cut up
2 medium potatoes
1 large onion, chopped (1 cup)
¾ cup chicken broth (see tip, page 36)
1 clove garlic, minced
½ teaspoon dried thyme, crushed
1 cup whipping cream
¾ cup milk
3 tablespons dry white wine *or* dry sherry

To clean live oysters, scrub shells under cold running water, using a stiff brush. Open oysters over bowl to catch liquid and oysters (see photo 1, Oysters). In a large saucepan cook bacon over medium-low heat for 6 to 8 minutes or till crisp, stirring often. Remove bacon; drain and reserve *2 tablespoons* bacon drippings in the saucepan (see photo 2).

Drain oysters, reserving ½ cup liquor; add water, if necessary, to make ½ cup. Add raw oysters and reserved liquor to reserved drippings. Cook 3 to 4 minutes or till edges of oysters curl, stirring frequently (see photo 3). Set aside.

Peel and dice potatoes (see photo 4). In a large saucepan combine potatoes, onion, chicken broth, garlic, thyme, ¼ teaspoon *pepper,* and ⅛ teaspoon *salt.* Bring to boiling. Reduce heat, then simmer, covered, about 20 minutes or till potatoes are tender. Stir in cream and milk. Bring just to boiling. Add cooked (or canned) oysters and their liquor and wine. Heat through, stirring occasionally. Season. Ladle into bowls. Sprinkle with bacon. Trim with parsley, if desired. Makes 3 main-dish or 4 side-dish servings.

New England Clam Chowder: Prepare Elegant Oyster Stew as above, *except* substitute 1-pint shucked *clams,* chopped, *or* two 7½-ounce cans minced *clams* for the oysters. Cook the fresh shucked clams for 2 to 3 minutes.

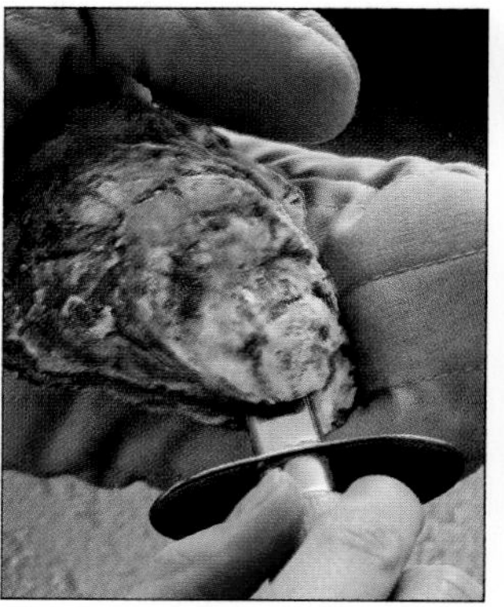

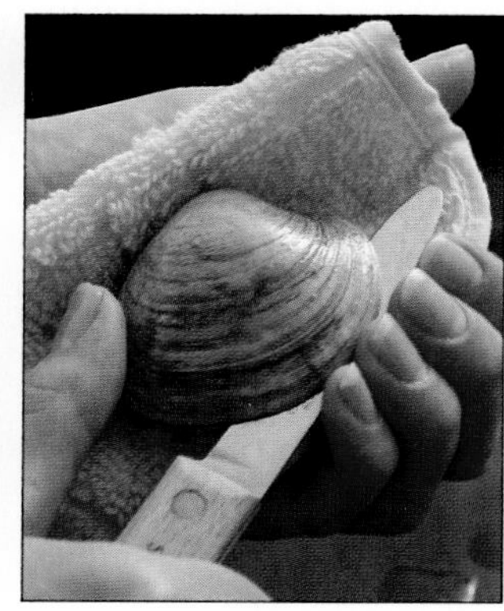

1 Oysters: For easier shucking, chill oysters before opening. To shuck, hold oyster in an oven mitt or heavy hot pad with flat side up. Using a strong-bladed oyster knife with a hand guard, insert knife tip into hinge between shells, as shown. Twist blade to pry oyster open; move blade along inside of upper shell, freeing muscle. Slide knife under oyster to cut from bottom shell. Discard any bits of shell.

Clams: Soak the clams in salted water. Chill for easier shucking. Working over a plate to catch any juices, hold clam with hinged side against a heavy cloth in one palm. Insert a sturdy blunt-tip knife between shell halves, as shown. Holding the shell firmly, move knife blade around clam, cutting the muscles that hold the shell together. Twist knife slightly to pry shell open. Cut clam muscle free from the shell. Discard any pieces of shell.

2 After cooking the bacon, remove the small pieces with a slotted spoon. Place on paper towels and let drain, as shown. Leave a couple tablespoons of the bacon drippings in the saucepan. The drippings add extra flavor to the seafood stew.

Manhattan Clam Chowder

For a quicker-to-fix chowder, replace the clams in the shell with a pint of shucked clams or two 7½-ounce cans of minced clams.

24 clams, chilled
3 slices bacon, cut up
1 medium green pepper, chopped (¾ cup)
1 medium onion, chopped (½ cup)
1 stalk celery, chopped (⅓ cup)
1 medium potato
3 cups water
1 16-ounce can tomatoes, cut up
1 8-ounce can tomato sauce
1 medium carrot, finely chopped (½ cup)
1 teaspoon dried thyme, crushed
¼ teaspoon salt
¼ teaspoon pepper

To clean live clams, scrub shells under cold running water, using a stiff brush. For soaking, in a Dutch oven combine 4 quarts *cold water* and ⅓ cup *salt;* add clams. Soak 15 minutes; drain and rinse. Discard water. Repeat soaking, draining, and rinsing twice. Open clams and remove from shells (see photo 1, Clams). In a large saucepan cook bacon over medium-low heat for 6 to 8 minutes or till crisp, stirring often. Remove bacon; drain and reserve *2 tablespoons* bacon drippings in the saucepan (see photo 2).

Coarsely chop shucked clams; set aside. Strain juice to remove bits of shell; reserve ⅔ cup. If using shucked or canned clams, drain juice; if necessary, add water to equal ⅔ cup. Set aside. Add green pepper, onion, and celery to drippings in saucepan. Cook till vegetables are tender, stirring frequently.

Peel and dice potato (see photo 4). Add potato, water, tomatoes, tomato sauce, carrot, thyme, salt, and pepper to saucepan. Bring to boiling. Reduce heat, then simmer, covered, for 30 to 35 minutes. Stir in clams, reserved juice, and bacon. Heat through, stirring occasionally. Ladle into soup bowls. Makes 4 main-dish or 8 side-dish servings.

3 Before cooking, the raw oyster looks very plump and soft (see top spoon). After cooking, the edges of the oyster curl (see bottom spoon).

4 To dice potatoes, slice peeled potatoes ⅛ to ¼ inch thick. Cut slices into ⅛- to ¼-inch-wide strips. Pile strips together and cut crosswise into even cubes, as shown. The cubes will measure ⅛ to ¼ inch on each side.

Pleasing Poultry Soups

Years ago a campaign slogan promised "a chicken in every pot." Today's promise—tasty poultry soups in every pot.

We've packed our soups with flavor by simmering poultry, vegetables, and just the right amounts of seasonings.

Simmer a soup and savor a spoonful. We're sure you'll agree that we've kept our promise. These poultry soups are downright delicious.

Turkey-Vegetable Soup

Turkey-Vegetable Soup

You should get about 3 cups of turkey off the turkey frame. If the frame doesn't yield that much, toss in extra bite-size pieces of cooked turkey.

1 meaty turkey frame
8 cups water
4 stalks celery, cut up
1 large yellow onion with skin, cut into wedges
1 tablespoon instant chicken bouillon granules
1 teaspoon salt
1 teaspoon dried thyme, crushed
8 to 10 whole black peppers
1 bay leaf
4 medium carrots, sliced (2 cups)
12 ounces broccoli

Break turkey frame or cut frame apart with the kitchen shears; separate the breast from the back and cut breast and back pieces in half so that all the pieces will fit into the Dutch oven. Place turkey pieces in a large Dutch oven. Add water, celery, onion, bouillon granules, salt, thyme, peppers, and bay leaf (see photo 1). Bring to boiling. Reduce heat, then simmer, covered, for 1½ hours.

Remove the large pieces of turkey frame (see photo 2). Strain broth (see photo 3). Discard vegetables and seasonings. Remove fat from broth (see photos 4 and 5, page 35). When bones are cool enough to handle, remove turkey from bones and coarsely chop. Set aside.

Return broth to Dutch oven and stir in carrots. Bring to boiling. Reduce heat, then simmer, covered, for 5 minutes.

Meanwhile, cut up broccoli into flowerets and measure 2 cups (see photo 4). Reserve stems for another use. Add broccoli flowerets to Dutch oven. Return to boiling; cook, covered, 6 to 7 minutes more or till vegetables are tender. Add turkey; heat through (see photo 5). Ladle into soup bowls. Makes 6 main-dish servings.

1 To prevent the soup from boiling over, start with a Dutch oven or stockpot that's the right size. Add the poultry, liquid, cut-up vegetables, and seasonings.

2 Use tongs or a slotted spoon to remove the large, bony poultry pieces. Place the pieces in a bowl to drain. Let cool while straining and removing fat from the broth.

3 For a clear broth, strain broth through a sieve lined with clean cheesecloth for cooking. Lift the cheesecloth out of the sieve, as shown, and discard.

4 Remove the floweret parts of the broccoli stems. Then, cut the flowerets into bite-size pieces. Save the broccoli stems to use in another soup or salad recipe.

5 Add the cut-up cooked meat near the end of simmering so it doesn't break up or overcook. If you get less than 3 cups cut-up turkey for 6 main-dish servings, add some extra cooked turkey

Chicken and Vegetable Stew

Use thighs or drumsticks when dark meat is preferred and breast portions when light meat is desired. Or, if it doesn't matter, use a combination of these pieces.

3 pounds meaty chicken pieces
4 cups water
1 large onion, cut into wedges
1 tablespoon Worcestershire sauce
1 teaspoon salt
¼ teaspoon pepper
¼ teaspoon bottled hot pepper sauce
1 16-ounce can tomatoes, cut up
1 15-ounce can tomato puree
2 medium potatoes, peeled and cubed
1 10-ounce package frozen whole kernel corn
1 10-ounce package frozen lima beans

Place chicken in a Dutch oven. Add water, onion, Worcestershire sauce, salt, pepper, and hot pepper sauce. Bring to boiling. Reduce heat, then simmer, covered, for 1 hour or till chicken is tender.

Remove chicken pieces (see photo 2, page 64). Strain broth (see photo 3, page 64). Discard onion. Remove fat from broth (see photos 4 and 5, page 35). When chicken is cool enough to handle, remove chicken from bones and coarsely chop. Discard skin and bones. Set chicken aside.

Return broth to Dutch oven and stir in *undrained* tomatoes, tomato puree, cubed potatoes, corn, and lima beans. Bring to boiling. Reduce heat, then simmer, covered, about 25 minutes or till vegetables are done. Add chicken; heat through (see photo 5, page 65). If desired, season to taste. Ladle into soup bowls. Makes 8 main-dish servings.

Curried Chicken-Rice Soup

1 pound meaty chicken pieces
3 cups water
1 cup apple juice
1 medium onion, cut into wedges
1 medium carrot, cut up
1 stalk celery, cut up
2 teaspoons curry powder
1 teaspoon salt
1 teaspoon lemon juice
2 whole cloves
¼ cup long grain rice
1 large tart apple, peeled, cored, and chopped
Snipped parsley *or* cilantro (optional)

Place chicken in a Dutch oven. Add water, apple juice, onion, carrot, celery, curry powder, salt, lemon juice, and cloves. Bring to boiling. Reduce heat, then simmer, covered, for 1 hour or till chicken is very tender.

Remove chicken pieces (see photo 2, page 64). Strain broth (see photo 3, page 64). Discard vegetables. Remove fat from broth (see photos 4 and 5, page 35). When chicken is cool enough to handle, remove chicken from bones and coarsely chop. Discard skin and bones. Set chicken aside.

Return broth to Dutch oven and stir in *uncooked* rice. Bring to boiling. Reduce heat, then simmer, covered, for 10 minutes. Add apple and simmer, covered, for 5 minutes more. Add chicken; heat through (see photo 5, page 65). Ladle into soup bowls. Sprinkle each serving with snipped parsley or cilantro, if desired. Makes 2 or 3 main-dish servings.

Chicken Wonton Soup

One taste panel member exclaimed "It's chicken noodle soup with an Oriental twist!"

2 pounds meaty chicken pieces
Gingerroot
8 cups water
1 medium yellow onion with skin, cut into wedges
1 large carrot, cut up
3 cloves garlic, halved
1 teaspoon salt
¼ teaspoon pepper
1 16-ounce package loose-pack frozen mixed green beans, broccoli, mushrooms, and red peppers
¼ cup soy sauce
8 wonton skins *or* 2 egg roll skins, cut into thin strips, *or* 1 cup medium noodles

Place chicken in a Dutch oven. Cut a 1-inch piece of gingerroot ½ inch thick. Add gingerroot, water, onion, carrot, garlic, salt, and pepper to chicken in Dutch oven. Bring to boiling. Reduce heat, then simmer, covered, for 1 hour or till chicken is tender.

Remove chicken pieces (see photo 2, page 64). Strain broth (see photo 3, page 64). Discard vegetables and seasonings. Remove fat from broth (see photos 4 and 5, page 35). When chicken is cool enough to handle, remove chicken from bones and coarsely chop. Discard skin and bones. Set chicken aside.

Return broth to Dutch oven and stir in frozen mixed vegetables and soy sauce. Bring to boiling. (If using noodles, add at this point.) Reduce heat, then simmer, covered, for 5 minutes. Add wonton or egg roll skin strips. Simmer, covered, for 5 minutes more or till the vegetables are tender. Add chicken; heat through (see photo 5, page 65). Ladle into soup bowls. Makes 6 main-dish servings.

Turkey Tortellini Soup

1 4-pound turkey hindquarter *or* turkey legs
8 cups water
4 sprigs parsley
1 large clove garlic, halved
2 teaspoons Italian seasoning
1 teaspoon salt
1 14½-ounce can tomatoes, cut up
1 9-ounce package frozen Italian green beans
1 small zucchini, thinly sliced (about 1 cup)
1 7-ounce package frozen cheese tortellini
Grated Parmesan cheese

Place turkey in a large Dutch oven. Add water, parsley, garlic, Italian seasoning, and salt. Bring to boiling. Reduce heat, then simmer, covered, for 2 hours or till turkey is tender.

Remove large pieces of turkey (see photo 2, page 64). Strain broth (see photo 3, page 64). Discard vegetables. Remove fat from broth (see photos 4 and 5, page 35). When turkey is cool enough to handle, remove turkey from bones and coarsely chop (should have about 4 cups turkey). Discard bones. Set turkey aside.

Return broth to Dutch oven and stir in *undrained* tomatoes, beans, zucchini, and tortellini. Bring to boiling. Reduce heat, then simmer, covered, for 5 to 10 minutes or till pasta and vegetables are done. Add turkey; heat through (see photo 5, page 65). Ladle into soup bowls. Pass cheese. Makes 8 main-dish servings.

Best of Bean Soups

For those who don't know beans about dry beans, here's your chance to bone up on the subject. We'll "show and tell" you how to do some simple bean cookery.

Select a dry bean variety—pinto, navy, lima, or great northern. Then, bubble a potful of luscious-tasting soup following a recipe from this chapter.

Lima-Sesame Soup

Lima-Sesame Soup

1 cup dry lima beans
4 cups water
4 cups Vegetable Stock (see recipe, page 37) *or* vegetable broth (see tip, page 36)
2 medium carrots, bias sliced (1 cup)
1 medium onion, chopped (½ cup)
1 clove garlic, minced
¼ teaspoon dry mustard
2 tablespoons sesame seed
1 teaspoon grated gingerroot
2 tablespoons butter *or* margarine
2 tablespoons soy sauce
2 tablespoons dry sherry
10 ounces romaine, torn, *or*
16 ounces bok choy, cut into ¾-inch pieces (about 6 cups)

Rinse dry beans (see photo 1). In a Dutch oven combine beans and water. Soak beans by either the quick or overnight soaking methods (see tip, right). Drain and rinse beans (see photo 2).

Return beans to the Dutch oven. Add Vegetable Stock or vegetable broth, sliced carrots, chopped onion, garlic, and mustard. Bring to boiling. Reduce heat, then simmer, covered, for 25 minutes or till beans are tender, stirring occasionally (see photo 3).

Meanwhile, in a small skillet cook sesame seed and gingerroot in butter or margarine about 1 minute or till seeds are toasted (see photo 4). Stir in soy sauce and dry sherry. Add sesame mixture to soup. Stir in romaine or bok choy, *one-fourth* at a time. Cook, uncovered, for 5 minutes more. Ladle into soup bowls. Makes 8 side-dish servings.

1 Place the dry beans in a colander or sieve. Then, rinse the beans under cold running tap water, as shown. Discard the damaged beans and any foreign material found in the beans.

Soaking Beans

Quick soaking method: In a Dutch oven bring beans and measured amount of water to boiling. Reduce heat; simmer, uncovered, for 2 minutes. Remove from heat; cover and let stand for 1 hour.

Overnight soaking method: Combine beans and measured amount of cold water. Cover container. Let stand in a cool place for 6 to 8 hours or overnight. Or, if room is warm, soak beans in the refrigerator.

2 Drain the soaked beans in a colander or sieve, discarding the soaking liquid. Then, rinse the beans thoroughly under running tap water.

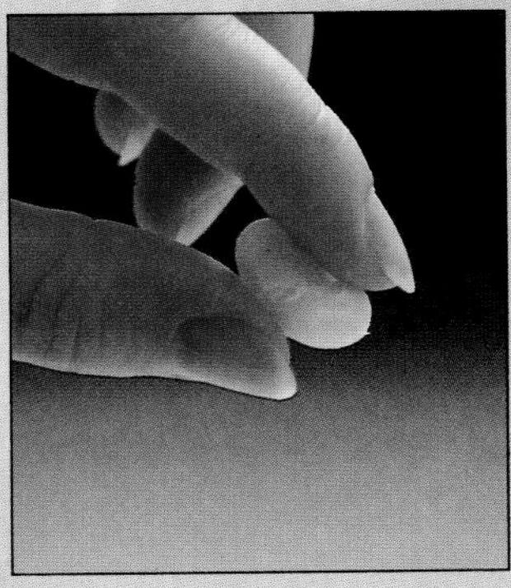

3 To test beans for doneness, remove a bean from the saucepan. Press it between your thumb and finger. The beans are done when they feel soft. If there is a hard core, cook the beans a little longer and test again.

4 Toast the sesame seed in butter or margarine in a small skillet. Toasting changes the color of the sesame seed to a golden brown and brings out the nutty flavor.

Creamy Northern Bean Soup

Extra delicious when dolloped with Basil Pesto. You'll find the recipe in the tip on page 43.

1 pound dry great northern beans
6 cups water
4 cups water
2 cups shredded cabbage
2 medium carrots, shredded (1 cup)
1 medium turnip, peeled and diced
1 medium onion, chopped (½ cup)
1 teaspoon salt
1 teaspoon instant chicken bouillon granules
1 teaspoon dried oregano, crushed
½ teaspoon dried marjoram, crushed
2 bay leaves
¼ teaspoon pepper
2 cups milk

Rinse dry beans (see photo 1, page 70). In a Dutch oven combine beans and the 6 cups water. Soak beans by either the quick or overnight soaking methods (see tip, page 70). Drain and rinse beans (see photo 2, page 71).

Return beans to the Dutch oven. Add the 4 cups water, cabbage, carrots, turnip, onion, salt, chicken bouillon granules, oregano, marjoram, bay leaves, and pepper. Bring to boiling. Reduce heat, then simmer, covered, for 1½ to 2 hours or till beans are tender, stirring occasionally (see photo 3, page 71).

Discard bay leaves. Mash beans slightly. Stir in milk and heat through. Season to taste. Ladle into soup bowls. Makes 6 main-dish servings.

Crockery Cooker Directions: Rinse beans. Soak beans in the 6 cups water by the overnight soaking method (see tip, page 70). Drain and rinse beans. In a 3½- or 4-quart electric slow crockery cooker combine beans and remaining ingredients *except* milk. Cover and cook on high heat setting for 6 to 8 hours. Stir in milk. Cover and cook 10 to 15 minutes more or till hot. Discard bay leaves. Season to taste.

Lima-Broccoli Soup

Smoked turkey sausage tastes similar to Polish sausage.

1¼ cups dry lima beans
4 cups water
4 cups water
1 medium onion, chopped (½ cup)
½ teaspoon salt
¼ teaspoon pepper
1 16-ounce can tomatoes, cut up
8 ounces smoked turkey sausage, cut into ½-inch-thick slices and halved
1 cup loose-pack frozen cut broccoli

Rinse dry beans (see photo 1, page 70). In a Dutch oven combine beans and 4 cups water. Soak beans by either the quick or overnight soaking methods (see tip, page 70). Drain and rinse beans (see photo 2, page 71).

Return beans to the Dutch oven. Add 4 cups water, onion, salt, and pepper. Bring to boiling. Reduce heat, then simmer, covered, 20 minutes.

Add *undrained* tomatoes. Simmer, covered, 15 minutes longer. Add sausage and broccoli. Return to boiling. Reduce heat, then simmer, covered, about 5 minutes or till broccoli is tender. Season to taste. Ladle into soup bowls. Makes 6 main-dish servings.

Cheese-Bean Chowder

- 1½ cups dry pinto beans *or* dry navy beans
- 4 cups water
- 4 cups beef broth (see tip, page 36)
- 1 medium onion, chopped (½ cup)
- 1 stalk celery, chopped (½ cup)
- ½ teaspoon dried basil, crushed
- 1 bay leaf
- 2 cups milk
- 2 cups shredded process American cheese (8 ounces)
- Snipped parsley

Rinse dry beans (see photo 1, page 70). In a Dutch oven combine beans and water. Soak beans by either the quick or overnight soaking methods (see tip, page 70). Drain and rinse beans (see photo 2, page 71).

Return beans to the Dutch oven. Add beef broth, onion, celery, basil, and bay leaf. Bring to boiling. Reduce heat, then simmer, covered, for 2½ to 3 hours or till beans are tender, stirring occasionally (see photo 3, page 71).

Discard bay leaf. Mash beans slightly. Stir in milk and cheese. Cook and stir till cheese melts and soup is heated through. Ladle into soup bowls. Garnish with snipped parsley. Makes 5 main-dish servings.

Crockery Cooker Directions: Rinse beans. Soak beans in the water by the overnight soaking method (see tip, page 70). Drain and rinse beans. In a 3½- or 4-quart electric slow crockery cooker combine beans and remaining ingredients *except* milk and cheese. Cover and cook on high heat setting for 6 to 8 hours. Stir in milk and cheese. Cover and cook 10 to 15 minutes more or till heated through. Discard bay leaf. Serve as above.

Sausage-Navy Bean Stew

- 1 pound dry navy beans (2⅓ cups)
- 6 cups water
- 4½ cups Beef Stock (see recipe, page 36) *or* beef broth (see tip, page 36)
- 1 pound Italian sausage links, cut into ½-inch-thick slices
- 3 cups chopped cabbage
- 1 16-ounce can tomatoes, cut up
- 1 large onion, chopped (1 cup)
- 1 clove garlic, minced
- 1 teaspoon dried oregano, crushed
- 2 bay leaves
- ½ teaspoon salt
- ¼ teaspoon pepper

Rinse dry beans (see photo 1, page 70). In a Dutch oven combine beans and water. Soak by either the quick or overnight soaking methods (see tip, page 70). Drain and rinse beans (see photo 2, page 71).

Return beans to the Dutch oven. Add Beef Stock or beef broth, sausage slices, cabbage, *undrained* tomatoes, onion, garlic, oregano, bay leaves, salt, and pepper. Bring to boiling. Reduce heat, then simmer, covered, for 2½ to 3 hours or till beans are tender, stirring occasionally (see photo 3, page 71). Discard bay leaves. Ladle into bowls. Makes 6 main-dish servings.

Crockery Cooker Directions: Rinse beans. Soak beans in the 6 cups water by the overnight soaking method (see tip, page 70). Drain and rinse beans. In a 3½- or 4-quart electric slow crockery cooker combine beans and remaining ingredients. Cover and cook on high heat setting for 6 to 8 hours. Discard bay leaves.

Chili Bonanza

Ask 10 chili cooks for their favorite chili recipe and you'll probably get 10 different recipes. Some think chili should be made with ground meat—others start with meat cubes. Some include beans; others omit them altogether.

Even the spice level varies. Some make a mild and nicely calm chili and others pack a powerful punch into their specialties.

Here you'll find five varieties—one's sure to suit your taste.

Chorizo Chili

Chorizo Chili

Anaheim peppers also are called California green chili peppers. They possess a mild flavor, with just a slight peppery bite.

½ pound chorizo, broken into chunks, *or* Italian sausage links, sliced
¾ pound beef round steak, cut into ½-inch cubes
1 large onion, chopped (1 cup)
1 large clove garlic, minced
6 anaheim peppers *or* two 4-ounce cans diced green chili peppers, drained
1 large green pepper
4 cups Beef Stock (see recipe, page 34) *or* beef broth (see tip, page 36)
2 tablespoons paprika
1 tablespoon dried oregano, crushed
1 teaspoon ground cumin
½ teaspoon ground red pepper
2 16-ounce cans hominy, drained
1 cup shredded cheddar cheese (4 ounces)
Tortilla chips

In a Dutch oven brown chorizo or Italian sausage. Remove with a slotted spoon; set aside. Cook beef, onion, and garlic in drippings till meat is brown (see photo 1). Drain off fat; set aside. Select anaheim or canned chili peppers, then seed and chop anaheim peppers and green pepper (see photo 2).

Stir chorizo or Italian sausage, anaheim or chili peppers, green pepper, Beef Stock or beef broth, paprika, oregano, cumin, and red pepper into Dutch oven with browned beef mixture. Bring to boiling. Reduce heat, then simmer, covered, about 1½ hours; stir occasionally. If necessary, remove excess fat from chili mixture (see photo 3). Stir hominy into chili. Then, simmer, uncovered, 10 minutes more; stir occasionally.

To serve, spoon chili into soup bowls. Sprinkle shredded cheese atop chili in each bowl. Serve with tortilla chips. Makes 4 main-dish servings.

1 When browning the meat, stir the meat with a spoon for even browning. For larger quantities of meat (1½ pounds or more) brown half the meat at a time. (Break up ground meat as it browns.)

2 Select fresh or canned peppers. If using fresh anaheim peppers (the long, narrow peppers shown), wear gloves or cover your hand with a plastic bag and avoid contact with skin or eyes. Remove seeds. Cut pepper into strips and chop.

3 To remove excess fat from the chili, tilt the pan slightly to collect the oily looking liquid at the edge of the pan. Then skim off the fat using a metal spoon; discard the fat.

Hot and Spicy Chili

Pickled jalapeño peppers add the spicy wallop!

1 pound ground beef *or* ground pork
1 large onion, chopped (1 cup)
2 pickled jalapeño peppers
1 28-ounce can tomatoes, cut up
3 cups tomato juice
2 tablespoons chili powder
½ teaspoon salt
1 bay leaf
2 15-ounce cans garbanzo beans, drained

In a Dutch oven cook beef or pork and onion till meat is brown and onion is tender (see photo 1, page 76). Drain off fat. Return meat and vegetables to pan.

Rinse, seed, and chop jalapeño peppers (see photo 2, page 77). (Should have about 2 tablespoons chopped peppers.) Stir chopped peppers, *undrained* tomatoes, tomato juice, chili powder, salt, and bay leaf into Dutch oven with browned meat mixture. Bring to boiling. Reduce heat, then simmer, covered, about 1½ hours; stir occasionally.

If necessary, remove excess fat from chili mixture (see photo 3, page 77). Stir in drained garbanzo beans. Simmer, covered, 30 minutes more; stir occasionally. Discard bay leaf. Ladle into soup bowls. If desired, sprinkle shredded cheddar cheese atop each serving. Makes 6 main-dish servings.

Texas-Style Chili

1 pound beef round steak, cut into ½-inch cubes
2 tablespoons cooking oil
1 pound boneless pork shoulder, cut into ½-inch cubes
2 to 3 tablespoons chili powder
2 tablespoons cornmeal
1½ teaspoons ground cumin
1 teaspoon dried oregano, crushed
¼ to ½ teaspoon ground red pepper
3 cloves garlic, minced
1⅓ cups water
1 10½-ounce can condensed beef broth
4 cups cooked pinto beans (*or* canned pinto beans, heated and drained)
Dairy sour cream
Lime wedges

In a Dutch oven brown beef in hot oil (see photo 1, page 76). Remove from pan. Brown pork in remaining hot oil. Drain meat.

Return all meat to pan. Stir in chili powder, cornmeal, cumin, oregano, red pepper, and garlic. Then stir in water and condensed broth. Bring to boiling. Reduce heat, then simmer, covered, about 1½ hours or till meat is tender; stir occasionally. If necessary, remove excess fat from chili mixture (see photo 3, page 77).

To serve, spoon meat mixture atop pinto beans in soup bowls. Dollop each serving with sour cream and drizzle with a little lime juice. Makes 8 main-dish servings.

Crockery Cooker Directions: In a large skillet cook beef in hot oil till brown; remove. Cook pork in hot oil till brown. Drain beef and pork. In a 3½- to 4-quart electric slow crockery cooker combine browned meats, chili powder, cornmeal, cumin, oregano, red pepper, garlic, water, and condensed broth. Cover and cook on low-heat setting for 8 to 10 hours or on high-heat setting for 4 to 5 hours. Serve meat atop beans as above.

Three-Bean Chili-Beer Soup

The ever-popular marinated bean salad was our inspiration for this flavorful chili.

1½ pounds ground beef
1 large onion, chopped (1 cup)
1 large green pepper, chopped (1 cup)
1 28-ounce can tomatoes, cut up
2 12-ounce cans beer
1½ cups beef broth (see tip, page 36)
1 15½-ounce can red kidney beans, drained
1 15-ounce can garbanzo beans, drained
1 15-ounce can pinto beans, drained
1 4-ounce can diced green chili peppers, drained
2 tablespoons chili powder
1½ teaspoons ground cumin
1½ teaspoons dried basil, crushed
1 teaspoon salt
Dairy sour cream

In a large Dutch oven cook half of the beef till brown; remove and drain off fat. Cook remaining beef, onion, and green pepper till meat is brown and vegetables are tender (see photo 1, page 76). Drain off fat. Return all meat and vegetables to pan.

Stir in *undrained* tomatoes, beer, beef broth, kidney beans, garbanzo beans, pinto beans, chili peppers, chili powder, cumin, basil, and salt. Bring to boiling. Reduce heat, then simmer, covered, about 1 hour; stir occasionally.

If necessary, remove excess fat from chili mixture (see photo 3, page 77). To serve, ladle into soup bowls and top each serving with a dollop of sour cream. Makes 8 main-dish servings.

Turkey Chili With Pasta

Reminiscent of the classic Mexican sauce mole, this chili has a spicy cocoa sauce that imparts a fascinating flavor.

2 pounds ground turkey
1 large onion, chopped (1 cup)
3 cloves garlic, minced
2 tablespoons chili powder
1 teaspoon crushed red pepper
2 16-ounce cans tomatoes, cut up
1 cup water
2 tablespoons unsweetened cocoa powder
1 teaspoon ground cumin
½ teaspoon salt
1 15½-ounce can red kidney beans
1¼ cups macaroni (4 ounces)
1 cup shredded cheddar cheese (4 ounces)

In a Dutch oven cook half the turkey till brown; remove from pan. Cook remaining turkey, onion, and garlic till turkey is brown and onion is tender (see photo 1, page 76). Drain off fat, if necessary. Return all meat and onion to pan.

Stir in chili powder and crushed red pepper. Then, stir in *undrained* tomatoes, water, cocoa powder, cumin, and salt. Bring to boiling. Reduce heat, then simmer, covered, for 50 minutes; stir occasionally. Add *undrained* beans. Bring to boiling. Reduce heat, then simmer, covered, 10 minutes more.

Meanwhile, cook macaroni according to package directions till done (see photo 4, page 19). Serve chili in soup bowls over cooked macaroni. Sprinkle each serving with cheese. Makes 6 main-dish servings.

Incredibly Creamy Soups

Meat and potatoes . . . cake and ice cream . . . peanut butter and jelly. What do these foods all have in common? They're famous food pairs, just like soup and crackers.

On the next few pages, you'll find some cream-of-the-crop soups. Each is a perfect noontime or suppertime partner for any chilly day meal.

Sausage-Cheese Chowder

Sausage-Cheese Chowder

- 1 cup small broccoli flowerets
- ¾ cup water
- 1 medium carrot, coarsely shredded
- 1 stalk celery, chopped (½ cup)
- 1 small onion, chopped (¼ cup)
- ¼ cup butter *or* margarine
- ¼ cup all-purpose flour
- 2 cups milk
- 8 ounces smoked Polish sausage, cut into thin slices
- 1½ cups shredded American cheese (6 ounces)
- ¾ cup beer

In a small saucepan combine broccoli, water, carrot, celery, and onion. Bring to boiling. Reduce heat, then simmer, covered, for 8 to 10 minutes or till tender. *Do not drain.*

Meanwhile, in a large saucepan melt butter or margarine. Stir in flour (see photo 1). Add milk (see photo 2). Cook and stir till thickened and bubbly (see photo 3).

If desired, halve sausage slices. Stir sausage, cheese, and beer into thickened mixture. Stir over low heat till cheese melts and sausage is heated (see photo 4). Stir in *undrained* vegetables; heat through. Ladle into soup bowls. Makes 4 main-dish servings.

Microwave Directions: In a 1-quart microwave-safe casserole combine broccoli, water, carrot, celery, and onion. Micro-cook, covered, on 100% power (HIGH) for 3 to 4 minutes or till vegetables are just tender. Set aside. In a 2-quart microwave-safe casserole place butter or margarine. Micro-cook, uncovered, on 100% power (HIGH) for 45 to 55 seconds or till melted. Stir in flour and milk. Micro-cook, uncovered, on 100% power (HIGH) for 5 to 6 minutes or till thickened and bubbly, stirring each minute till the mixture starts to thicken, then stirring every 30 seconds. Stir in sausage, cheese, beer, and *undrained* vegetables. Micro-cook, uncovered, on 100% power (HIGH) for 2 to 3 minutes or till hot and cheese is melted.

1 Our cream soup base starts as a simple white sauce. To make a smooth sauce, stir flour into the melted butter till no lumps remain in the mixture.

2 Add the liquid all at once to the fat-flour mixture. Once the liquid is added, stir the sauce constantly to evenly distribute the fat-flour mixture throughout the liquid.

3 Cook over medium heat, stirring constantly so that the sauce is evenly heated. Continue cooking till mixture bubbles across the entire surface, as shown.

4 Turn the heat to low before adding cheese and other ingredients. Stir the mixture till the cheese is melted and soup is heated through. Stir occasionally so the soup doesn't stick or scorch.

Cream of Tomato Soup

4 or 5 medium tomatoes, chopped (2½ cups), *or* one 16-ounce can tomatoes, chopped
1 stalk celery, chopped (½ cup)
1 small onion, chopped (⅓ cup)
⅓ cup tomato paste
1 bay leaf
½ teaspoon sugar
3 tablespoons butter *or* margarine
3 tablespoons all-purpose flour
3 cups milk

In a medium saucepan combine *undrained* tomatoes, celery, onion, tomato paste, bay leaf, and sugar. Bring to boiling. Reduce heat, then simmer, covered, for 18 to 20 minutes or till celery and onion are very tender. Discard bay leaf. Place mixture in a blender container or food processor bowl. Cover and blend or process till smooth. Strain mixture through a sieve; set aside. (You should have 1¾ cups.)

Meanwhile, in a large saucepan melt butter or margarine. Stir in flour, ½ teaspoon *salt,* and ⅛ teaspoon *pepper* (see photo 1, page 82). Add milk (see photo 2, page 83). Cook and stir till thickened and bubbly (see photo 3, page 83). Gradually stir in tomato mixture; heat through. Ladle into bowls. Sprinkle with snipped chives, if desired. Makes 3 or 4 side-dish servings.

Attention, Microwave Owners!

Recipes with microwave directions were tested in countertop microwave ovens that operate on 600 to 700 watts. Times are approximate because microwave ovens vary by manufacturer.

Elegant Chicken and Asparagus Soup

Dovetail the recipe preparation by cooking asparagus on the range top or in the microwave oven at the same time you cook the creamy soup base on the range top.

1 10-ounce package frozen cut asparagus
1 cup Veal Stock (see recipe, page 37) *or* chicken broth (see tip, page 36)
⅓ cup sliced green onion
¼ teaspoon dried tarragon, crushed
⅛ teaspoon ground coriander
⅛ teaspoon white pepper
3 tablespoons butter *or* margarine
¼ cup all-purpose flour
2 cups Veal Stock (see recipe, page 37) *or* chicken broth (see tip, page 36)
1 cup light cream *or* milk
2 cups diced cooked chicken *or* turkey

In a saucepan combine asparagus, 1 cup Veal Stock or chicken broth, green onion, tarragon, coriander, and pepper. Bring to boiling. Reduce heat, then simmer, covered, for 8 minutes or till asparagus is tender. *Do not drain.*

Meanwhile, in a large saucepan melt butter or margarine. Stir in flour (see photo 1, page 82). Add 2 cups Veal Stock or chicken broth and cream or milk (see photo 2, page 83). Cook and stir till thickened and bubbly (see photo 3, page 83). Stir in *undrained* asparagus mixture and cooked chicken or turkey; heat through. Season to taste with salt. Ladle into soup bowls. Makes 4 main-dish servings.

Microwave Directions: In a 1-quart microwave-safe casserole combine asparagus, 1 cup Veal Stock or chicken broth, green onion, tarragon, coriander, and pepper. Micro-cook, covered, on 100% power (HIGH) for 5 to 7 minutes or till asparagus is tender, stirring once to break up. Set aside. Proceed as above, cooking soup on the range top.

Tuna-Corn Chowder

3 tablespoons butter *or* margarine
1 small onion, chopped (1/4 cup)
1/4 cup all-purpose flour
1/2 teaspoon dried dillweed
1/4 teaspoon pepper
2 cups milk
2 cups Chicken Stock (see recipe, page 36) *or* chicken broth (see tip, page 36)
1/2 teaspoon Worcestershire sauce
1 12-ounce can whole kernel corn with sweet peppers *or* whole kernel corn, drained
1 9 1/4-ounce can tuna, drained and broken into chunks

In a large saucepan melt butter or margarine. Cook onion in butter or margarine till tender but not brown. Stir in flour, dillweed, and pepper (see photo 1, page 82). Add milk, Chicken Stock or chicken broth, and Worcestershire sauce (see photo 2, page 83). Cook and stir till thickened and bubbly (see photo 3, page 83). Stir in corn and tuna; heat through. Ladle into soup bowls. Sprinkle with snipped parsley, if desired. Makes 4 main-dish servings.

Cream of Potato Soup

2 medium potatoes, cubed (1 1/2 cups)
1 1/2 cups Vegetable Stock (see recipe, page 37) *or* chicken broth (see tip, page 36)
1/4 cup butter *or* margarine
1 medium onion, chopped (1/2 cup)
1/2 cup chopped green pepper
1/4 cup all-purpose flour
1/4 teaspoon pepper
1/8 teaspoon salt
2 cups milk

In a saucepan combine potatoes and Vegetable Stock or chicken broth. Bring to boiling. Reduce heat, then simmer, covered, about 10 minutes or till tender. *Do not drain.*

Meanwhile, in a large saucepan melt butter or margarine. Cook onion and green pepper in butter or margarine till tender but not brown. Stir in flour, pepper, and salt (see photo 1, page 82). Add milk (see photo 2, page 83). Cook and stir till thickened and bubbly (see photo 3, page 83). Stir in *undrained* potatoes. Heat through. Ladle into soup bowls. Sprinkle with snipped parsley, if desired. Makes 4 side-dish servings.

Creamy Taco Soup

1 pound lean ground beef
1 large onion, chopped (1 cup)
1/4 cup butter *or* margarine
1/3 cup all-purpose flour
1 1 1/4-ounce envelope taco seasoning mix
4 cups Beef Stock (see recipe, page 34) *or* beef broth (see tip, page 36)
2 cups milk
1 15 1/2-ounce can red kidney beans, drained
1 14 1/2-ounce can tomatoes, cut up
1 cup shredded Monterey Jack cheese (4 ounces)
Crushed corn chips
Dairy sour cream

In a Dutch oven cook ground beef and onion till meat is brown and onion is tender (see photo 1, page 76). Drain off fat. Remove meat mixture from saucepan; set aside.

In the same pan melt butter or margarine. Stir in flour (see photo 1, page 83). Add taco seasoning mix, Beef Stock or beef broth, and milk (see photo 2, page 83). Cook and stir till thickened and bubbly (see photo 3, page 83).

Stir in beans, *undrained* tomatoes, and meat mixture. Heat through. Stir over low heat till cheese melts (see photo 4, page 83). Ladle into soup bowls. Pass corn chips and sour cream. Makes 6 main-dish servings.

Cauliflower-Crab Chowder

- **1 10-ounce package frozen cauliflower**
- **½ cup water**
- **3 tablespoons butter *or* margarine**
- **3 tablespoons all-purpose flour**
- **1¾ cups Vegetable Stock (see recipe, page 37), Chicken Stock (see recipe, page 36), *or* chicken broth (see tip, page 36)**
- **1¼ cups milk**
- **1 3-ounce package cream cheese with chives, cubed**
- **2 tablespoons chopped pimiento**
- **2 tablespoons snipped parsley**
- **¼ teaspoon salt**
- **1 6-ounce package frozen crab meat, thawed and drained**
- **¼ cup dry white wine**

In a medium saucepan combine cauliflower and water. Bring to boiling. Reduce heat, then simmer, covered, about 4 minutes or just till crisp-tender. *Do not drain.* Cut up large pieces of cauliflower; set aside.

Meanwhile, in a large saucepan melt butter or margarine. Stir in the flour (see photo 1, page 82). Add Vegetable Stock, Chicken Stock, or chicken broth and milk (see photo 2, page 83). Cook and stir till thickened and bubbly (see photo 3, page 83).

Stir in *undrained* cauliflower, cream cheese, pimiento, parsley, and salt. Stir over low heat till cheese melts (see photo 4, page 83). Stir in crab; heat through. Stir in wine. Immediately ladle into soup bowls. Makes 3 main-dish servings.

Microwave Directions: In a 1-quart microwave-safe casserole combine cauliflower and water. Micro-cook, covered, on 100% power (HIGH) for 7 to 9 minutes or till crisp-tender, stirring once to break apart. *Do not drain.* Cut up large pieces of cauliflower. Set aside. In a 2-quart microwave-safe casserole place butter or margarine. Micro-cook, uncovered, on 100% power (HIGH) for 40 to 50 seconds or till melted. Stir in flour. Add Vegetable Stock, Chicken Stock, or chicken broth and milk. Micro-cook, uncovered, on 100% power (HIGH) for 8 to 10 minutes or till thickened and bubbly, stirring each minute till the mixture starts to thicken, then stirring every 30 seconds. Stir in the *undrained* cauliflower, cheese, pimiento, parsley, and salt. Micro-cook 3 minutes more. Stir till cheese is melted. Stir in crab. Micro-cook 1 to 2 minutes more or till heated through. Stir in wine. Serve as above.

Wild-Rice Soup

- **¼ cup wild rice**
- **1½ cups Veal Stock (see recipe, page 37) *or* chicken broth (see tip, page 36)**
- **1 medium onion, chopped (½ cup)**
- **1 stalk celery, sliced (½ cup)**
- **½ teaspoon dried thyme, crushed**
- **3 tablespoons butter *or* margarine**
- **¼ cup all-purpose flour**
- **⅛ teaspoon pepper**
- **2 cups milk**
- **1 cup Veal Stock (see recipe, page 37) *or* chicken broth (see tip, page 36)**
- **½ teaspoon Worcestershire sauce**
- **2 tablespoons snipped parsley**

Run cold tap water over rice in a strainer about 1 minute, lifting rice to rinse well. In a medium saucepan combine rice, 1½ cups Veal Stock or chicken broth, onion, celery, and thyme. Bring to boiling. Reduce heat, then simmer, covered, for 45 minutes or till rice is done.

Meanwhile, in a large saucepan melt butter or margarine. Stir in flour and pepper (see photo 1, page 82). Add milk and 1 cup Veal Stock or chicken broth (see photo 2, page 83). Cook and stir till thickened and bubbly (see photo 3, page 83). Stir in rice mixture and Worcestershire sauce. Heat through. Ladle into bowls. Sprinkle with parsley. Makes 4 side-dish servings.

▶ *Cauliflower-Crab Chowder*

Full-House Stews

When stew has the leading role on the menu at your house, you'll fill every seat at the table. Why? Because the wonderful cooking aromas preview the delectable stew to come.

Mouth-watering meats, a variety of vegetables, and a well-flavored gravy simmer into a flavorful stew that is sure to get rave reviews.

Serve any of these steaming stews. Then, sit back and enjoy the accolades.

Country-Style Pork Stew

Country-Style Pork Stew

- ¾ pound lean boneless pork
- 2 cloves garlic, minced
- 1 tablespoon cooking oil
- 1½ cups Chicken Stock (see recipe, page 36) *or* chicken broth (see tip, page 36)
- 2 small onions, cut into wedges
- 1 7½-ounce can tomatoes, cut up
- 1 stalk celery, sliced (½ cup)
- 1 teaspoon dried oregano, crushed
- 1 teaspoon ground cumin
- ¼ teaspoon salt
- 1 small yellow summer squash *or* zucchini, halved lengthwise and cut into ½-inch-thick slices
- 1 9-ounce package frozen cut green beans *or* ¾ pound fresh wax beans *or* green beans, cut into 1-inch pieces
- 3 tablespoons cold water
- 1 tablespoon cornstarch

Cut meat into ¾-inch cubes (see photo 1). In a large saucepan or a Dutch oven cook meat and garlic in hot oil till meat is brown (see photo 1, page 76).

Stir in Chicken Stock or broth, onions, *undrained* tomatoes, celery, oregano, cumin, and salt. Bring to boiling. Reduce heat, then simmer, covered, about 1 hour or till meat is tender.

Stir in squash and frozen beans.* Bring mixture to boiling. Reduce heat, then simmer, covered for 5 minutes more. If necessary, skim off fat from stew (see photo 3, page 77).

Combine cold water and cornstarch (see photo 2). Stir cornstarch mixture into stew, then cook and stir till thickened and bubbly (see photo 3). Cook and stir 2 minutes more. Ladle stew into bowls. Makes 3 or 4 main-dish servings.

***Note:** If using fresh beans, stir into stew without the squash. Bring mixture to boiling. Reduce heat, then simmer, covered, for 10 to 15 minutes. Stir in squash and simmer 5 minutes more. Continue as above.

1 Trim excess fat from the meat. To make cubes easily, cut meat into ¾-inch-thick slices. Then, cut the slices into ¾-inch pieces. Steady the meat as you cut.

2 In a small bowl stir liquid into the cornstarch (or flour) until mixture is smooth. Use a wire whisk if you have difficulties getting rid of all the lumps.

3 Gradually add the cornstarch or flour mixture to the stew. Be sure to stir while adding the thickening. Continue to stir during cooking so that the mixture doesn't stick or get lumpy.

Oven Beef Stew

1½ pounds beef stew meat, cut into ¾-inch cubes
3 tablespoons cooking oil
3 cups Beef Stock (see recipe, page 34) *or* beef broth (see tip, page 36)
1 large onion, chopped (1 cup)
1 teaspoon dried savory, crushed
1 teaspoon dried thyme, crushed
½ teaspoon salt
¼ teaspoon garlic powder
¼ teaspoon pepper
½ cup cold water
¼ cup all-purpose flour
1 10-ounce package frozen succotash
3 medium carrots, cut into 1-inch pieces
3 medium potatoes, peeled and cut into 1-inch pieces

In a Dutch oven brown meat, half at a time, in hot oil (see photo 1, page 76). Drain off fat. Return all meat to the pan.

Stir in Beef Stock or beef broth, onion, savory, thyme, salt, garlic powder, and pepper. Bring to boiling. Remove from heat. Cover tightly and bake in a 325° oven for 45 minutes. Combine cold water and flour (see photo 2, page 90). Stir flour mixture into stew (see photo 3, page 91).

Add succotash, carrots, and potatoes to stew. Bake, covered, for 1¼ hours more or till meat and vegetables are tender and mixture is thickened. Ladle stew into bowls. Season to taste. Makes 6 main-dish servings.

Crockery Cooker Directions: Brown meat in hot oil as above. Drain off fat. In a 3½- to 4-quart electric slow crockery cooker combine *2½ cups* Beef Stock or beef broth, onion, *¾ teaspoon* savory, thyme, salt, garlic powder, pepper, succotash, carrots, and potatoes. Stir in meat. Cover and cook on low-heat setting for 9 to 11 hours or on high-heat setting for 4½ to 5½ hours. Combine remaining *½ cup* Beef Stock or beef broth and flour (omit the cold water); stir into stew. Cover and cook on high-heat setting for 30 minutes or until bubbly.

Oriental-Style Chicken Stew

Although it's an optional step, removing all the chicken bones before you thicken the stew makes eating the stew much easier . . . and it takes only a few minutes.

4 large chicken thighs (about 1¼ pounds)
2 tablespoons cooking oil
1¼ cups Chicken Stock (see recipe, page 36) *or* chicken broth (see tip, page 36)
½ cup dry white wine *or* chicken broth
½ of a 6-ounce can (⅓ cup) frozen pineapple juice concentrate, thawed
2 tablespoons soy sauce
⅛ teaspoon pepper
1 large sweet red pepper *or* green pepper, cut into ½-inch pieces
2 cups sliced fresh mushrooms
¼ cup cold water
2 tablespoons cornstarch
1 6-ounce package frozen pea pods *or* 2 cups fresh pea pods, halved diagonally
2 cups hot cooked rice

Remove skin from chicken. In a large saucepan brown chicken in hot oil. Drain off fat.

Stir in 1¼ cups Chicken Stock or chicken broth, wine or chicken broth, pineapple juice concentrate, soy sauce, and pepper. Bring to boiling. Reduce heat, then simmer, covered, about 25 minutes or till chicken is almost tender.

Add red or green pepper and mushrooms. Bring mixture to boiling. Reduce heat, then simmer, covered, about 5 minutes more or till pepper is crisp-tender. If desired, remove chicken thighs from stew, then remove meat from bones. Discard bones.

Combine cold water and cornstarch (see photo 2, page 90). Stir cornstarch mixture into stew, then cook and stir till thickened and bubbly (see photo 3, page 91). Add pea pods and chicken pieces. Cook and stir 2 minutes more. Ladle stew into bowls with hot cooked rice. Makes 4 main-dish servings.

Mideastern Lamb Stew

Couscous (KOOS koos) is a semolina pasta that's very tiny. Prepare it according to package directions.

1 pound lean boneless lamb
2 tablespoons olive oil *or* cooking oil
2½ cups Beef Stock (see recipe, page 34) *or* beef broth (see tip, page 36)
1 8-ounce can tomato sauce
1 large onion, chopped (1 cup)
1 tablespoon lemon juice
1 clove garlic, minced
½ teaspoon ground turmeric
½ teaspoon ground cumin
¼ teaspoon salt
¼ teaspoon pepper
1 small eggplant (about 1 pound), peeled and cut into ¾-inch cubes (4 cups)
1 large tomato, peeled and chopped
1 large green pepper, chopped (1 cup)
¼ cup raisins
⅓ cup cold water
3 tablespoons all-purpose flour
2 cups hot cooked couscous *or* buttered noodles

Cut meat into ¾-inch cubes (see photo 1, page 90). In a Dutch oven brown meat in hot olive or cooking oil (see photo 1, page 76). Drain off fat.

Stir in Beef Stock or beef broth, tomato sauce, onion, lemon juice, garlic, turmeric, cumin, salt, and pepper. Bring to boiling. Reduce heat, then simmer, covered, for 30 minutes.

Stir in eggplant, tomato, green pepper, and raisins. Bring to boiling. Reduce heat, then simmer, covered, about 30 minutes more or till meat and vegetables are tender. If necessary, skim off fat from stew (see photo 3, page 77).

Combine cold water and flour (see photo 2, page 90). Stir flour mixture into stew, then cook and stir till thickened and bubbly (see photo 3, page 91). Cook and stir 1 minute more. Ladle stew into bowls and serve with couscous or buttered noodles. Makes 4 main-dish servings.

Lamb and Garbanzo Stew

The best cut to select for lean lamb is meat from the leg.

1 pound lean boneless lamb
2 tablespoons cooking oil
1 10¾-ounce can condensed chicken broth
1 large onion, chopped (1 cup)
1 clove garlic, minced
1½ teaspoons dried thyme, crushed
1 teaspoon Worcestershire sauce
¼ teaspoon pepper
1 16-ounce can tomatoes, cut up
1 15-ounce can garbanzo beans, drained
½ cup cold water
3 tablespoons all-purpose flour
¼ cup snipped parsley

Cut meat into ¾-inch cubes (see photo 1, page 90). In a Dutch oven brown meat in hot oil (see photo 1, page 76). Drain off fat.

Stir in condensed chicken broth, onion, garlic, thyme, Worcestershire sauce, and pepper. Bring to boiling. Reduce heat, then simmer, covered, for 30 minutes.

Stir in *undrained* tomatoes and drained garbanzo beans. Bring to boiling. Reduce heat, then simmer, covered, about 30 minutes more or till meat is tender. If necessary, skim off fat from stew (see photo 3, page 77).

Combine cold water and flour (see photo 2, page 90). Stir flour mixture into stew, then cook and stir till thickened and bubbly (see photo 3, page 91). Cook and stir 1 minute more. Stir in parsley. Ladle stew into bowls. Makes 4 main-dish servings.

Autumn Beef Stew

2 slices bacon
1 pound beef stew meat *or* venison, cut into ¾-inch cubes
3 cups Beef Stock (see recipe, page 34) *or* beef broth (see tip, page 36)
1 medium onion, chopped (½ cup)
¾ cup apple cider *or* apple juice
1 tablespoon vinegar
½ teaspoon salt
½ teaspoon dried marjoram, crushed
¼ teaspoon pepper
2 cups peeled winter squash cut into ½-inch cubes (about 10 ounces)
1 medium parsnip, sliced ¼ inch thick (1 cup)
1 large apple, cored and sliced
¼ cup raisins (optional)
½ cup apple cider *or* apple juice
¼ cup all-purpose flour

In a Dutch oven cook bacon till crisp. Remove bacon; drain, crumble, and set aside. Reserve drippings in Dutch oven. In Dutch oven brown beef or venison in hot bacon drippings (see photo 1, page 76). Drain off fat.

Stir in Beef Stock or beef broth, onion, ¾ cup apple cider or apple juice, vinegar, salt, marjoram, and pepper. Bring to boiling. Reduce heat, then simmer, covered, about 1½ hours or till meat is nearly tender.

Stir in squash; parsnip; apple; raisins, if desired; and crumbled bacon. Bring to boiling. Reduce heat, then simmer, covered, for 10 minutes more or till vegetables are tender. If necessary, skim off fat from stew (see photo 3, page 77).

Combine ½ cup apple juice or cider, and flour (see photo 2, page 90). Stir flour mixture into stew, then cook and stir till thickened and bubbly (see photo 3, page 91). Cook and stir 1 minute more. Ladle stew into bowls. Makes 4 main-dish servings.

Snappy Tomato-Veal Stew

¾ pound boneless veal
1 clove garlic, minced
1 tablespoon cooking oil
2 12-ounce cans vegetable juice cocktail
1 large onion, chopped (1 cup)
½ teaspoon dried basil, crushed
¼ teaspoon salt
¼ teaspoon pepper
1 medium parsnip, sliced (1 cup)
1 cup sliced fresh mushrooms
1 cup coarsely chopped cabbage
1 large stalk celery, sliced (⅔ cup)
2 small potatoes, cut into ¾-inch pieces
¼ cup cold water
2 tablespoons all-purpose flour

Cut meat into ¾-inch cubes (see photo 1, page 90). In a Dutch oven cook meat and garlic in hot oil till meat is brown (see photo 1, page 76). Drain off fat.

Stir in vegetable juice cocktail, onion, basil, salt, and pepper. Bring to boiling. Reduce heat, then simmer, covered, for 30 minutes.

Stir in parsnip, mushrooms, cabbage, celery, and potatoes. Bring to boiling. Reduce heat, then simmer, covered, for 20 to 30 minutes more or till meat and vegetables are tender. If necessary, skim off fat (see photo 3, page 77).

Combine cold water and flour (see photo 2, page 90). Stir flour mixture into stew, then cook and stir till thickened and bubbly (see photo 3, page 91). Cook and stir 1 minute more. Ladle stew into bowls. Makes 4 main-dish servings.

▶ *Autumn Beef Stew*

Dumplings Ahoy!

"Ahoy, mate! Islands ahead!" Our "islands" are fluffy dumplings floating atop a "sea" of stew.

Make your own dumpling discovery—choose curry or caraway, potato or cheese.

How about sailing off to your kitchen? You're on your way to locating some new, uncharted dumpling-topped stews.

Lamb Stew with Curried Cornmeal Dumplings

Lamb Stew With Curried Cornmeal Dumplings

1 pound lean boneless lamb
2 tablespoons cooking oil
2 cups water
¾ teaspoon dried marjoram, crushed
¼ teaspoon pepper
⅓ cup all-purpose flour
⅓ cup cornmeal
1 teaspoon baking powder
½ teaspoon curry powder
1 slightly beaten egg yolk
¼ cup milk
2 tablespoons cooking oil
3 tablespoons all-purpose flour
1 10-ounce package frozen peas
2 cups fresh mushrooms, halved
1 cup frozen small whole onions

Cut meat into ¾-inch cubes (see photo 1, page 90). In a 12-inch skillet or a Dutch oven brown meat in 2 tablespoons hot oil (see photo 1, page 76). Drain off fat.

Stir in water, marjoram, pepper, and ¾ teaspoon *salt*. Bring to boiling. Reduce heat, then simmer, covered, for 50 minutes.

For dumplings, in a mixing bowl stir together ⅓ cup flour, cornmeal, baking powder, curry powder, and ¼ teaspoon *salt*. Combine egg yolk, milk, and 2 tablespoons oil, then add to flour-cornmeal mixture, stirring with a fork just till combined (see photo 1).

Combine ¼ cup *cold water* and 3 tablespoons flour (see photo 2, page 90). Stir flour mixture into stew, then cook and stir till thickened and bubbly (see photo 3, page 91). Add peas, mushrooms, and onions. Return to boiling.

Drop the dumpling mixture from a tablespoon to make 4 large mounds atop the bubbling stew (see photo 2). Cover and simmer for 10 to 12 minutes (see photo 3). Test dumplings for doneness (see photo 4). Ladle stew and dumplings into bowls. Makes 4 main-dish servings.

1 Stir the dry ingredients together to distribute them evenly. Then add the combined liquid ingredients. Stir with a fork just till mixed. Don't overmix or the dumplings will be heavy.

2 Drop the dumpling dough atop the bubbly stew. The stew should be boiling so that the bottom of the dumpling gets evenly cooked.

3 Cover the pan and cook the dumplings till done. Keep the pan covered until the minimum cooking time. (Don't even peek.)

4 To check the dumplings for doneness, insert a wooden toothpick into one of the dumplings. It should come out clean when the dumpling is done.

Chicken Stew with Potato Dumplings

2½ pounds meaty chicken pieces
2 stalks celery, sliced (1 cup)
1 medium onion, chopped (½ cup)
2 tablespoons instant chicken bouillon granules
½ teaspoon dried rosemary, crushed
2 bay leaves
1 medium potato, peeled and cut up
1 tablespoon butter *or* margarine
2 beaten eggs
⅓ cup all-purpose flour
1 teaspoon dried parsley flakes
½ teaspoon baking powder
¼ teaspoon onion salt
½ cup all-purpose flour
1 16-ounce package frozen mixed vegetables

In a Dutch oven combine chicken, celery, onion, bouillon granules, rosemary, bay leaves, 4½ cups *water,* ½ teaspoon *salt,* and ¼ teaspoon *pepper.* Bring to boiling. Reduce heat, then simmer, covered, for 1 hour. Remove chicken from broth. Discard bay leaves. When chicken is cool enough to handle, remove meat from bones; cut up chicken. Discard skin and bones. Skim fat from broth.

For dumplings, in a saucepan cook potato in boiling water for 15 to 20 minutes or till tender. Drain well. Add butter or margarine. Mash potato and stir in eggs till smooth. Combine ⅓ cup flour, parsley, baking powder, and onion salt. Stir into mashed potato till thoroughly mixed. Set aside.

Combine 1 cup *cold water* and ½ cup flour (see photo 2, page 90). Stir flour mixture into broth in Dutch oven. Stir in frozen vegetables. Cook and stir till thickened and bubbly (see photo 3, page 91). Add chicken. Return to boiling. Drop the dumpling mixture from a spoon to make 12 small dumplings atop the bubbling mixture (see photo 2, page 98). Cover and simmer for 12 to 15 minutes (see photo 3, page 99). Test dumplings for doneness (see photo 4, page 99). Ladle into bowls. Makes 6 main-dish servings.

Pork and Cabbage Stew with Dumplings

1 pound lean boneless pork
1 tablespoon cooking oil
2 cups water
1½ cups apple juice
1 large onion, chopped (1 cup)
1 tablespoon Worcestershire sauce
1 teaspoon dried thyme, crushed
¼ teaspoon salt
¼ teaspoon pepper
3 cups coarsely chopped cabbage
3 large carrots, cut into ½-inch-thick slices
1 cup packaged biscuit mix
¼ teaspoon caraway seed
⅓ cup milk
¼ cup cold water
2 tablespoons all-purpose flour
Paprika (optional)

Cut meat into ¾-inch cubes (see photo 1, page 90). In a Dutch oven brown meat in hot oil (see photo 1, page 76).

Stir in 2 cups water, apple juice, onion, Worcestershire sauce, thyme, salt, and pepper. Bring to boiling. Reduce heat, then simmer, covered, for 30 minutes. Stir in cabbage and carrots. Cover and simmer 20 minutes more or till meat and vegetables are nearly tender.

For dumplings, in a mixing bowl combine biscuit mix and caraway seed. Add milk all at once and stir till mixture is moistened (see photo 1, page 98).

Combine ¼ cup cold water and flour (see photo 2, page 90). Stir flour mixture into stew, then cook and stir till mixture is thickened and bubbly (see photo 3, page 91).

Drop the dumpling mixture from a tablespoon to make 4 mounds atop the bubbling stew (see photo 2, page 98). Cover and simmer 10 to 12 minutes (see photo 3, page 99). Test dumplings for doneness (see photo 4, page 99). Ladle into bowls and sprinkle dumplings with paprika, if desired. Makes 4 main-dish servings.

Beef and Zucchini Stew with Cheese Dumplings

1 pound beef stew meat, cut into ¾-inch cubes
2 tablespoons cooking oil
2 cups water
1 16-ounce can tomatoes, cut up
2 stalks celery, sliced (1 cup)
1 medium onion, chopped (½ cup)
1 clove garlic, minced
1 tablespoon instant beef bouillon granules
1 teaspoon dried oregano, crushed
¾ cup all-purpose flour
½ cup shredded cheddar cheese (2 ounces)
1½ teaspoons baking powder
⅛ teaspoon salt
1 beaten egg
¼ cup milk
1 tablespoon cooking oil
⅓ cup all-purpose flour
2 medium zucchini, cut into ½-inch-thick slices (3 cups)

In a Dutch oven brown meat in 2 tablespoons hot oil (see photo 1, page 76). Drain off fat. Stir in water, *undrained* tomatoes, celery, onion, garlic, bouillon granules, oregano, ½ teaspoon *salt,* and ⅛ teaspoon *pepper.* Bring to boiling. Reduce heat, then simmer, covered, for 1½ hours or till meat is tender.

For dumplings, in a mixing bowl stir together ¾ cup flour, *¼ cup* of the cheese, baking powder, and ⅛ teaspoon salt. Combine egg, milk, and 1 tablespoon oil, then add to flour-cheese mixture, stirring just till moistened (see photo 1, page 98).

Combine ¾ cup *cold water* and ⅓ cup flour (see photo 2, page 90). Stir flour mixture into stew, then cook and stir till thickened and bubbly (see photo 3, page 91). Add zucchini slices. Return to boiling.

Drop the dumpling mixture from a tablespoon to make 8 mounds atop the bubbling stew (see photo 2, page 98). Cover and simmer for 12 to 15 minutes (see photo 3, page 99). Test dumplings for doneness (see photo 4, page 99). Ladle stew and dumplings into bowls and sprinkle with remaining cheddar cheese. Makes 4 main-dish servings.

Surprising Spaetzle

Did you know that spaetzle (SHPETS luh) is a noodlelike dumpling? Try it instead of noodles the next time you make soup.

To make spaetzle, stir together 1 cup *all-purpose flour* and ½ teaspoon *salt.* Make a well in the center of the dry ingredients. Add a mixture of 1 beaten *egg* and ½ cup *milk;* mix well. Pour batter into a colander with large holes. Hold colander over boiling soup; press batter through. Simmer, uncovered, for 5 to 10 minutes or till done.

Stew with Baked-On Topper

Company coming for dinner? Serve them an elegant stew. Pastry-topped portions go from oven to table with little fuss.

Extra-special ingredients make this stew extraordinary—tender pieces of veal, fresh mushrooms, leeks, artichoke hearts, cream, and wine. Nothing but the best ingredients for your special guests!

Veal Stew with Pastry Topper

Veal Stew with Pastry Topper

2 pounds boneless veal
½ cup all-purpose flour
½ teaspoon salt
¼ teaspoon pepper
2 tablespoons cooking oil
4 cups mushrooms, quartered
4 medium leeks, thinly sliced (2 cups)
3 medium carrots, bias-sliced ½ inch thick (1¼ cups)
1½ cups Chicken Stock (see recipe, page 36), Veal Stock (see recipe, page 37), *or* chicken broth (see tip, page 36)
1 cup dry white wine
3 cloves garlic, minced
¾ teaspoon dried thyme, crushed
½ teaspoon dried rosemary, crushed
¼ teaspoon finely shredded lemon peel
2 egg yolks
½ cup whipping cream
1 9-ounce package frozen artichoke hearts, thawed and cut up
Rich Pastry
1 beaten egg

Cut meat into ¾-inch cubes (see photo 1, page 90). In a plastic bag combine ½ cup flour, salt, and pepper. Add meat cubes to flour mixture, a few at a time, shaking to coat. In a Dutch oven brown meat, half at a time, in hot oil. Add more oil, if necessary, to brown second half of meat. Return all meat to pan.

Stir in mushrooms, leeks, carrots, stock or broth, wine, garlic, thyme, rosemary, and lemon peel. Bring to boiling. Reduce heat, then simmer, covered, about 40 minutes or till meat is tender, stirring occasionally.

Beat together egg yolks and cream. Stir about *1 cup* of the hot mixture into egg yolk mixture (see photo 1). Return to hot mixture, stirring to combine. Stir in artichokes. Remove hot mixture from heat. Season to taste.

Meanwhile, prepare, roll out, and cut Rich Pastry (see photo 2). Divide meat mixture among six 14- or 16-ounce au gratin dishes or small casseroles. Place pastry over each casserole. Fold under extra pastry and flute to edge of dish (see photo 3). Brush pastry with beaten egg (see photo 4). Make decorative slits or cutouts in pastry for steam to escape. Add pastry cutouts made from scraps of pastry and brush with egg (see photo 5).

Transfer dishes to one or two baking sheets. Bake in a 450° oven for 10 to 12 minutes or till pastry is golden. Makes 6 main-dish servings.

Rich Pastry: In a mixing bowl combine 2 cups *all-purpose flour* and ½ teaspoon *salt.* Cut in ½ cup *shortening* and ¼ cup *cold butter or margarine* till mixture resembles coarse crumbs. Make a well in the center. Beat together 1 *egg yolk* and ¼ cup *cold water.* Add to flour mixture. Using a fork, stir till dough forms a ball. Divide dough in half. Wrap each ball in clear plastic wrap and chill 20 minutes in the freezer or 1½ hours in the refrigerator before rolling. On a lightly floured surface roll each half into a rectangle about ⅛ to ¼ inch thick; cut out three rounds or ovals measuring about ¾ to 1 inch larger than top of individual baking dishes.

2 Roll out half the pastry at a time on a lightly floured cloth or surface. Keep remaining pastry chilled. Using one of the baking dishes as a guide, cut the pastry $\frac{3}{4}$ to 1 inch larger than the top of the dish.

1 Stir some of the hot stew into the egg yolk mixture. By adding only a portion of the hot mixture, you'll gradually warm the eggs. (The yolks and cream help thicken the stew.)

3 To flute the pastry topper, press dough with the thumb of one hand against the thumb and forefinger of the other. Repeat around the baking dish.

4 Beat an egg in a small bowl or custard cup till combined. Brush pastry with the egg. The egg glazes the crust and gives it a special, golden appearance.

5 Make slits or cutouts in pastry for steam to escape. Decorate with pastry cutouts. One idea is to cut leaves, then score lightly to resemble veins. Add to pastry topper and brush with egg.

Gumbo With Gusto

"Gumbo" comes from the African word for okra. Yet, okra is only one of the many ingredients that goes into our wonderful soup. Another key ingredient is the browned flour-and-oil roux (ROO). The roux gives this gumbo its unique, rich flavor.

Serve the gumbo in the traditional way with a mound of rice in a flat soup bowl.

Gumbo

Gumbo

- 1 **pound fresh *or* frozen fish fillets**
- 1 **pound fresh *or* frozen shrimp in shells**
- ½ **cup all-purpose flour**
- ½ **cup cooking oil**
- 1 **large onion, chopped (1 cup)**
- 2 **stalks celery, chopped (1 cup)**
- 1 **medium green pepper, chopped (¾ cup)**
- 6 **cloves garlic, minced**
- 6 **cups Fish Stock (see recipe, page 36) *or* chicken broth (see tip, page 36)**
- 2 **cups sliced okra *or* one 10-ounce package frozen cut okra**
- 3 **bay leaves**
- 1 **teaspoon dried oregano, crushed**
- 1 **teaspoon dried thyme, crushed**
- 1 **teaspoon dried basil, crushed**
- ½ **teaspoon salt**
- ½ **teaspoon ground red pepper**
- 1 **pound andouille *or* smoked sausage, cut into ½-inch-thick slices**
- **Hot cooked rice**

Thaw fish and shrimp, if frozen. Remove skin from fish, if present; cut fish into 1-inch pieces (see photo 1, page 46). Peel and devein shrimp (see photo 1). Rinse. Chill fish and shrimp in the refrigerator till ready to use.

In a heavy Dutch oven stir together flour and oil till smooth (see photo 2). Cook over medium-low heat, *stirring constantly,* about 35 minutes or till a dark reddish brown roux is formed (see photo 3). Add onion, celery, green pepper, and garlic. Cook and stir over medium heat for 10 to 15 minutes or till vegetables are very tender. Gradually stir in Fish Stock or chicken broth. Stir in fresh or frozen okra, bay leaves, oregano, thyme, basil, salt, red pepper, and ¼ teaspoon *pepper.* Bring to boiling. Reduce heat, then simmer, covered, about 1 hour.

Add sausage and simmer 10 minutes (see photo 4). Add fish and shrimp and simmer about 5 minutes more or till fish flakes easily with a fork (see photo 3, page 47). Stir once. Discard bay leaves and spoon off fat. Season. Serve with rice. Makes 8 to 10 main-dish servings.

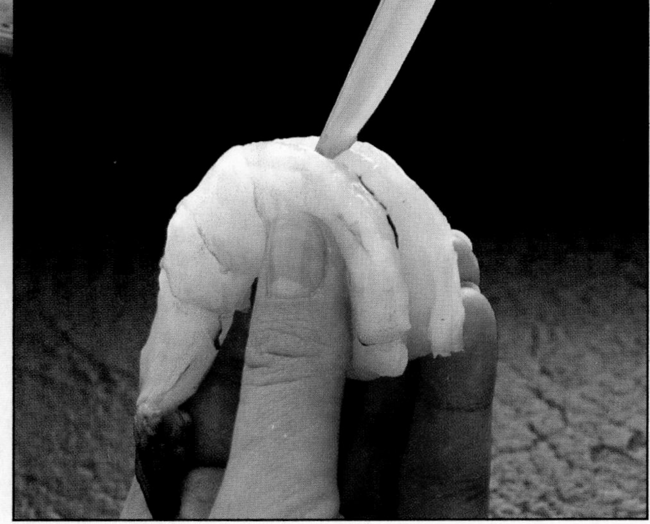

1 After peeling shrimp, make a shallow slit along the back from head end to tail end. Look for the black sand vein that runs along the center. If visible, use knife to carefully remove and discard it.

2 Use a wooden spoon to combine the flour and oil. Make sure the mixture is smooth. This is the start of the roux (ROO) that is used both for flavor and thickening in the gumbo. Note the light color of the mixture.

3 After you cook and stir the mixture over medium-low heat, the roux takes on a dark reddish-brown color, as shown. The color is sometimes compared to that of a tarnished copper penny.

4 Andouille (ahn DOO *ee*) is a pork sausage often used in a gumbo. Buy it in Louisiana area grocery stores or order it through the mail. Smoked sausage is a good substitute.

A Soup-Bar Party

Thinking about throwing a party? Our menu is a real knockout for an easy, yet impressive, supper.

With this buffet-style meal, you do some of the work ahead of time. In fact, the party plans are so streamlined, you'll enjoy the gathering as much as your guests will.

Menu

- Meatball Soup*
- Bibb Lettuce with Creamy Italian Dressing*
- Homemade bread or rolls* with butter
- Apple Dumplings with Raspberry Sauce*
- Beverages

*see pages 112-117

Meatball Soup

Meatball Soup

- 1 beaten egg
- ¼ cup milk
- 1 tablespoon prepared mustard
- ½ teaspoon salt
- Several dashes bottled hot pepper sauce
- 1 cup soft bread crumbs (1½ slices bread)
- 1 pound lean ground beef
- 4 ounces fresh spinach (2 cups)
- 2 large tomatoes
- 6 slices bacon
- 1 cup shredded mozzarella cheese (4 ounces)
- ½ cup grated Parmesan *or* Romano cheese
- ½ cup Croutons (optional)
- 8 cups Beef Stock (see recipe, page 34) *or* beef broth (see tip, page 36)
- 2½ cups tomato juice
- 1 cup tripolini (tiny bow-tie pasta)
- 2 cups sliced fresh mushrooms
- ½ cup thinly sliced green onions
- ¼ cup snipped parsley

For meatballs, in a bowl combine egg, milk, mustard, salt, and hot pepper sauce. Stir in bread crumbs. Add ground meat and mix well (see photo 1). Shape meat mixture into 48 meatballs (see photo 2). Place in a 13x9x2-inch baking pan. Bake in a 375° oven for 15 to 20 minutes. Drain well (see photo 3). (If desired, transfer baked meatballs to a bowl. Cover and chill till serving time.)

For soup toppers, cut spinach into fine strips (see photo 4). Cut tomatoes into ⅛- to ¼-inch pieces (see photo 5). Cook bacon till crisp; drain and finely crumble (see photo 6). Place spinach, tomatoes, bacon, cheeses, and croutons, if desired, into individual bowls.

In a Dutch oven combine Beef Stock or beef broth and tomato juice. Bring to boiling over medium-high heat. Add meatballs and pasta. Cook, uncovered, for 10 minutes or till pasta is tender. Stir in mushrooms and green onion and bring to boiling. Stir in parsley. Ladle immediately into soup bowls. Let guests select desired toppers. Makes 8 main-dish servings.

For 16 servings: Double all ingredients. Bake meatballs in a 15x10x1-inch baking pan. Use a large Dutch oven or soup kettle.

1 Mix the ground beef and egg mixture together lightly so that the meatballs will be light, not compact. Use your hands for mixing.

2 For evenly sized meatballs, pat the meat mixture into an 8x6-inch rectangle on a piece of waxed paper. Use a large knife to cut meat lengthwise and crosswise into 48 small squares of equal size. Then, roll each piece into a ball between both hands, as shown.

3 After baking, drain the meatballs on paper towels. Pat them with additional paper towels to remove as much fat as possible.

Soup Toppers

4 To make fine spinach strips, roll several spinach leaves together, then cut across into thin slices.

5 Core tomatoes. Slice tomatoes through stem end, making ⅛- to ¼-inch-thick slices. Cut each slice into ⅛- to ¼-inch pieces.

6 Crumble the drained, crisply cooked bacon into a small bowl. Use your fingers to break the bacon into small pieces.

Timetable

1 day before

- Bake one or more of the breads, depending on party size. Wrap the loaves and store at room temperature; wrap and freeze Crusty Onion Rolls. (Or, bake breads up to 4 months in advance. Wrap in moisture- and vaporproof wrap; freeze. On the day of the party, let frozen bread loaves stand at room temperature at least 4 hours to thaw. Frozen Crusty Onion Rolls can be thawed and crisped in the oven. See timings below.)
- Prepare the pastry for Apple Dumplings with Raspberry Sauce. Cut into squares and stack between waxed paper, as shown. Wrap and chill. Prepare sauce for dumplings; cover and chill.
- Prepare Creamy Italian Dressing; cover and chill.
- Bake meatballs for the Meatball Soup. Place in a bowl, then cover and chill in the refrigerator.

2 hrs. before

- (For the party serving 16, start preparations 2½ hours before.) Remove the pastry from the refrigerator. While the pastry warms, peel and core the apples, as shown. Keep the peeled apples in a bowl containing a mixture of lemon juice and water to prevent them from turning brown. Assemble the dumplings and chill.
- Place soup toppers in bowls; cover and chill.

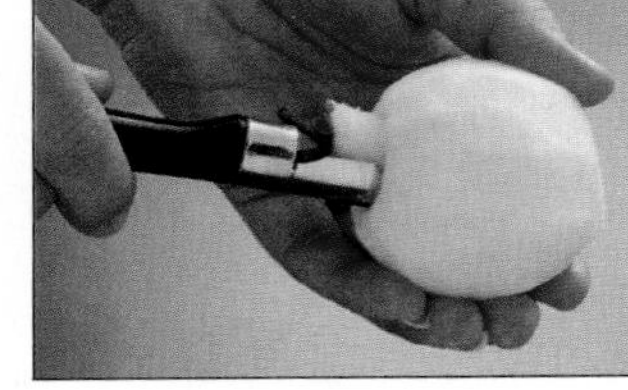

45 min. before

- Prepare the lettuce and place on a serving platter, as shown. Garnish the serving platter, if desired.
- Place foil-wrapped package of Crusty Onion Rolls on a baking sheet in a 375° oven. Bake for 25 minutes or till thawed. Uncover and bake 10 minutes more or till heated through and crusty.
- Meanwhile, start cooking the soup. Then, slice breads and cover; place on the table with butter.
- Prepare the coffee and tea.
- After your guests arrive, place the dumplings in the oven. They bake while your guests eat the soup, salad, and bread.

At Serving Time

- Set out the coffee, tea, soft drinks, and ice cubes for guests to help themselves.
- Ladle soup into a tureen, as shown. Or use an electric slow crockery cooker. Place container on serving table. Arrange the soup toppings on the table around the soup container. Place rolls, lettuce, and dressing on the buffet table.

Potato and Rye Bread

¼ cup cornmeal
½ cup buttermilk *or* milk
2 tablespoons butter *or* margarine
1 package active dry yeast
2 tablespoons honey
½ pound potatoes, peeled, cooked, and mashed (1 cup mashed)*
3¼ to 3¾ cups all-purpose flour
1 cup rye flour
Cornmeal
Butter *or* margarine, softened

In a small saucepan combine ¼ cup cornmeal and ¾ cup *water.* Bring to boiling. Cook and stir till thickened. Remove from heat; stir in buttermilk or milk, 2 tablespoons butter or margarine, and 1½ teaspoons *salt.* Cool. Dissolve yeast in ¼ cup *warm water* (110° to 115°); stir in honey. When cornmeal and mashed potatoes have cooled to warm (110° to 115°), combine with yeast mixture in a large bowl.

By hand, stir in *1½ cups* of the all-purpose flour and all of the rye flour. Turn out onto a lightly floured surface. Knead in enough remaining all-purpose flour to make a moderately stiff dough that is smooth and elastic (8 to 10 minutes total). (Dough will continue to absorb flour.)

Shape into a ball. Place in a lightly greased bowl; turn once to grease surface. Cover and let rise in a warm place till double (about 1½ hours). Punch dough down.

Divide dough in half. Cover and let rest for 10 minutes. Lightly grease two 8x4x2-inch loaf pans and sprinkle lightly with cornmeal. Shape each portion of dough into a loaf and place in the pans. With a sharp knife or kitchen scissors make three diagonal slashes across each loaf, about ¼ inch deep. Cover and let rise till nearly double (about 45 minutes).

Bake in a 375° oven about 40 minutes or till bread tests done. Cover with foil the last 10 minutes, if necessary, to prevent overbrowning. Remove loaves from pans immediately. Cool on a wire rack. Brush crusts with softened butter or margarine. Cool completely. Makes 2 loaves.

***Note:** To prepare mashed potatoes, peel and quarter the potatoes. Cook, covered, in boiling salted water for 20 to 25 minutes or till tender. Drain thoroughly. Mash with a potato masher or on low speed of an electric mixer.

Bibb Lettuce With Creamy Italian Dressing

1 cup mayonnaise *or* salad dressing
1 8-ounce carton dairy sour cream
2 green onions, chopped
2 tablespoons vinegar
2 teaspoons sugar
1 teaspoon Italian seasoning
¾ teaspoon celery salt
¾ teaspoon dry mustard
1 clove garlic, minced
4 small heads Bibb lettuce
Milk

For dressing, in a small mixing bowl combine mayonnaise or salad dressing, sour cream, onion, vinegar, sugar, Italian seasoning, celery salt, dry mustard, garlic, and ¼ teaspoon *pepper.* Use a wire whisk or rotary beater to mix till smooth. Transfer dressing to a container. Cover and chill till serving time.

Just before serving, cut each head of lettuce in half lengthwise. Arrange lettuce halves on a serving platter. If desired, garnish platter with cherry tomatoes or radishes and parsley sprigs. If necessary, stir 1 to 2 tablespoons milk into dressing till of desired consistency. Serve dressing with lettuce. Makes 8 servings.

For 16 servings: Double all ingredients.

Crusty Onion Rolls

5½ to 6 cups all-purpose flour
2 packages active dry yeast
2 cups water
1 tablespoon dried minced onion
1 tablespoon sugar
1 tablespoon shortening
2 teaspoons salt
½ cup finely chopped onion
3 tablespoons butter *or* margarine

In a large mixer bowl combine *2 cups* of the flour and yeast. In a saucepan heat water, dried onion, sugar, shortening, and salt just till warm (115° to 120°) and shortening is almost melted, stirring constantly. Add to flour mixture. Beat with an electric mixer on low speed for 30 seconds, scraping sides of bowl constantly. Beat on high speed for 3 minutes. Using a spoon, stir in as much of the remaining flour as you can.

Turn out onto a lightly floured surface. Knead in enough of the remaining flour to make a stiff dough that is smooth and elastic (8 to 10 minutes total). Shape into a ball. Place in a lightly greased bowl; turn once to grease surface. Cover and let rise in a warm place till double (45 to 60 minutes).

Punch dough down. Divide in half. Cover and let rest for 10 minutes. Cut each half of the dough into 10 pieces, making 20 pieces total. Shape into rolls. Place 2 inches apart on a greased baking sheet. Snip a shallow crisscross in tops of rolls with kitchen scissors. Cover and let rise till nearly double (40 to 45 minutes). Bake in a 375° oven for 25 minutes.

Meanwhile, cook chopped onion in butter till tender but not brown. Brush onion-butter mixture over tops of rolls. Continue baking 10 minutes longer or till onion is golden brown. Cool completely. Serve the same day. (Or, wrap in foil and freeze up to 4 months. Before serving, place foil-wrapped package on a baking sheet in a 375° oven for 25 minutes or till rolls are thawed. Uncover and bake 10 minutes or till heated through and crusty.) Makes 20 rolls.

Bran Batter Bread

Honey butter tastes great on slices of this hearty bread. To make the special butter, simply stir together two parts softened butter and one part honey.

1¼ cups whole wheat flour
½ cup bran flakes, crushed
¼ cup toasted wheat germ
1 package active dry yeast
1¼ cups buttermilk *or* sour milk
2 tablespoons brown sugar
2 tablespoons butter *or* margarine
¾ teaspoon salt
1 egg
1¼ cups all-purpose flour

In a large mixer bowl stir together whole wheat flour, bran flakes, wheat germ, and yeast. In a saucepan heat buttermilk or sour milk, brown sugar, butter or margarine, and salt just till warm (115° to 120°) and butter is almost melted, stirring constantly. Add to flour mixture; add egg. Beat with an electric mixer on low speed for 30 seconds, scraping sides of bowl constantly. Beat on high speed for 3 minutes. Using a spoon, stir in all-purpose flour, making a soft dough. Cover and let rise in a warm place till double (about 35 minutes).

Stir dough down. Spread in a greased 1½-quart casserole. Cover and let rise till nearly double (about 35 minutes).

Bake in a 375° oven for 40 to 45 minutes or till bread tests done, covering with foil the last 20 to 25 minutes, if necessary, to prevent overbrowning. Remove from dish. Cool on a wire rack. Makes 1 loaf.

Apple Dumplings With Raspberry Sauce

2¼ cups all-purpose flour
½ teaspoon salt
⅔ cup shortening
⅓ cup very finely chopped pecans
½ cup cold water
8 small apples, peeled and cored
Raisins, miniature semisweet chocolate pieces, chopped pecans, *or* chopped dates
Sugar
Ground cinnamon *or* ground nutmeg
Milk
Raspberry Sauce

For pastry, in a mixing bowl combine flour and salt; cut in shortening till pieces are the size of small peas. Stir in finely chopped pecans. Sprinkle *2 tablespoons* of the water over part of the mixture. Gently toss with a fork; push to side of the bowl. Repeat with remaining water till all is moistened. Form into a ball; divide in half.

On a lightly floured surface roll half of the dough into a 12-inch square. Using a fluted pastry wheel, cut into four 6-inch squares. Place dough squares in a stack, separating them with pieces of waxed paper. Repeat with remaining dough. Cover dough; chill for 1½ to 24 hours.

For dumplings, remove pastry from refrigerator; let stand 30 minutes at room temperature. Place an apple in the center of each dough square. Fill center of apple with raisins, chocolate pieces, chopped pecans, or dates. Sprinkle each with about *1 tablespoon* sugar; sprinkle with cinnamon or nutmeg. Moisten edges of pastry with water. Fold corners to center; pinch edges to seal. Place in a greased 15x10x1-inch baking pan. Brush dumplings with a little milk; sprinkle lightly with sugar. Bake in a 375° oven for 35 to 40 minutes or till pastry is brown. Serve with Raspberry Sauce. Makes 8 servings.

Raspberry Sauce: Thaw one 10-ounce package frozen *red raspberries.* In a saucepan combine 3 tablespoons *sugar* and 2 tablespoons *cornstarch.* Press thawed berries through a sieve to remove seeds. Stir sieved berries, 1 cup *cranberry juice cocktail,* and 1 tablespoon *butter or margarine* into sugar-cornstarch mixture. Cook and stir till mixture is thickened and bubbly, then cook and stir 2 minutes more. Cool about 30 minutes before serving. Makes 2 cups sauce.

For 16 servings: Prepare pastry as above, doubling all ingredients; divide dough into four pieces. Roll each piece into a 12-inch square. Cut each square into four 6-inch squares. Fill and wrap as above; place 10 dumplings in a greased 15x10x1-inch baking pan and 6 dumplings in a greased 13x9x2-inch baking pan. Bake as above. Double ingredients for sauce.

Hurray for Leftover Soup

Freeze or chill soup leftovers, and you'll have a quick meal for another day. (Don't freeze soups made with milk products.)

To reheat soup on the range top, use a covered saucepan over medium heat till mixture is heated throughout; stir often. Break up frozen soup during heating.

Microwave reheating is another option. Micro-cook frozen soup in a covered, microwave-safe container on 100% power (HIGH). Allow about 2½ minutes for ¾ cup, 3 to 4 minutes for 1 cup, 8 minutes for 1½ cups, and 10 minutes for 2 cups; stir once or twice. To micro-cook chilled soup, allow 2 minutes for ¾ cup, 3 minutes for 1 cup, 3 to 4 minutes for 1½ cups, and 5 minutes for 2 cups; stir once.

Soup Partners

Toppers and crackers make perfect accompaniments for homemade soups and stews. For toppers, float crunchy croutons, flavored popcorn, or crispy bread atop a soup. Or, match up home-baked crackers, such as dainty yeast crackers, hearty rye crackers, or delicate cheese wafers with a stew.

Pair these "partners" with your simmered soup favorites for an unbeatable team.

Herbed Croutons

For plain croutons, omit the herbs and garlic salt.

4 ½-inch-thick slices day-old white bread
3 tablespoons butter *or* margarine, melted, *or* cooking oil
½ teaspoon dried basil, crushed
¼ teaspoon dried oregano, crushed
¼ teaspoon dried thyme, crushed
¼ teaspoon onion powder
⅛ teaspoon garlic salt
⅛ teaspoon dried dillweed

Brush both sides of bread lightly with melted butter or margarine or oil. Cut into ½-inch cubes. Spread in a shallow baking pan. Toast in a 300° oven for 20 to 25 minutes or till bread cubes are dry and crisp, stirring occasionally.

Meanwhile, combine basil, oregano, thyme, onion powder, garlic salt, and dillweed. Sprinkle over hot toasted bread cubes. Toss to coat evenly. Cool. Store in a covered container in the refrigerator. Makes about 2½ cups.

Flavored Popcorn Toppers

Especially good on cream soups!

Cheese Popcorn: Melt 1 tablespoon *butter or margarine*. Drizzle over 2 cups *popped corn;* toss to mix. Add 1 tablespoon grated *Parmesan or Romano cheese* and toss to mix.

Onion Popcorn: Melt 1 tablespoon *butter or margarine;* stir in 1/4 teaspoon *onion salt*. Drizzle over 2 cups *popped corn;* toss to mix.

Garlic Popcorn: Melt 1 tablespoon *butter or margarine;* stir in 1/8 teaspoon *garlic salt*. Drizzle over 2 cups *popped corn;* toss to mix.

Herbed Popcorn: Melt 1 tablespoon *butter or margarine;* stir in 1/8 teaspoon dried *basil or oregano*, crushed. Drizzle over 2 cups *popped corn;* toss to mix.

Chili Popcorn: Melt 1 tablespoon *butter or margarine;* stir in 1/2 teaspoon *chili powder* and dash *bottled hot pepper sauce*. Drizzle over 2 cups *popped corn;* toss to mix.

Cheesy Garlic Crisps

A great topper on broth-type soups.

1/4 cup butter *or* margarine, melted
1 large clove garlic, minced
24 slices party rye bread *or* four 6-inch flour tortillas
1/4 cup grated Parmesan cheese

In a small mixing bowl combine melted butter or margarine and garlic. (If using tortillas, cut each into 6 wedges.) Brush one side of each rye bread slice or both sides of each tortilla wedge with some of the butter mixture. Place on a baking sheet. Bake in a 350° oven for 5 minutes. Turn over and sprinkle with cheese. Bake for 5 to 7 minutes more or till crisp and golden brown. Makes 24.

Garlic Crisps: Prepare the butter mixture and bread or tortilla wedges as above, *except* omit sprinkling with the Parmesan cheese.

Cheese Wafers

- 1 cup all-purpose flour
- ⅛ teaspoon dry mustard
- ⅛ teaspoon chili powder
- ⅛ teaspoon pepper
- 1 5-ounce jar American cheese spread
- ¼ cup butter *or* margarine

In a mixing bowl stir together flour, mustard, chili powder, and pepper. In a small mixer bowl beat cheese and butter or margarine together with an electric mixer till smooth. Beat in flour mixture till well combined, kneading in the last of the flour by hand, if necessary. Shape dough into roll 1½ inches in diameter. Wrap in waxed paper or clear plastic wrap. Chill in the refrigerator for 2 to 24 hours.

Remove from the refrigerator and reshape slightly to round out any flattened surfaces. Using a sharp knife, cut into ⅛-inch-thick slices. Place on an ungreased baking sheet. Bake in a 325° oven for 9 to 11 minutes or till lightly browned. Remove from baking sheet and place on a wire rack. Serve warm or cool. Store in an airtight container. Makes about 48 crackers.

Seeded Rye Crackers

- 1½ cups all-purpose flour
- 1 cup rye flour
- 2 tablespoons brown sugar
- 1½ teaspoons caraway seed
- 1 teaspoon baking powder
- ⅓ cup shortening
- ½ cup cold water

In a mixing bowl stir together all-purpose flour, rye flour, sugar, caraway seed, baking powder, and ¼ teaspoon *salt.* Cut in shortening till mixture resembles coarse crumbs. Add water all at once. Stir with a fork till mixture can be gathered into a ball. Turn out onto a lightly floured surface. Knead gently for 8 to 10 strokes.

On a lightly floured surface roll half the dough to 1/16- to ⅛-inch thickness. Cut into squares with a knife or pastry wheel, or cut into rounds with a 2½-inch biscuit cutter. Place on a lightly greased baking sheet. Repeat with remaining dough, rerolling as necessary. Prick crackers with a fork. Bake in a 325° oven for 10 to 15 mintues or till crisp. Remove from baking sheet and cool on a wire rack. Store in an airtight container. Makes about 48 crackers.

Yeast Crackers

Enjoy these crackers fresh from the oven. Or, reheat them in a 400° oven about 3 minutes to warm them.

2 cups all-purpose flour
1 package active dry yeast
¼ teaspoon baking soda
⅔ cup water
¼ cup shortening
½ teaspoon salt

In a small mixer bowl stir together *1 cup* of the flour, yeast, and soda. In a saucepan heat water, shortening, and salt just till warm (115° to 120°) and shortening is almost melted; stir constantly. Add to flour mixture. Beat with an electric mixer on low speed for 30 seconds, scraping bowl. Beat on high speed for 3 minutes.

Using a spoon, stir in as much of the remaining flour as you can. Turn out onto a lightly floured surface. Knead in remaining flour to make a stiff dough that is smooth and elastic (6 to 8 minutes total). If necessary, add 1 to 2 tablespoons flour to keep dough from sticking during kneading. Shape into a ball. Place in a lightly greased bowl; turn once to grease surface. Cover and let the dough rise in a warm place till double (about 45 minutes).

Punch dough down. Cover; let rest for 10 minutes. Roll dough to ¼-inch thickness. Dip a 1¾-inch round biscuit cutter into flour, then cut dough straight down. (Allow rolled dough to rest about 10 minutes before rerolling.) Place dough rounds on a greased baking sheet. Prick the tops of each 3 times with fork tines. (It's not necessary to let the dough rise before baking.)

Bake in a 400° oven for 10 to 15 minutes. Remove from baking sheet and place on a wire rack. Serve the crackers while warm. If desired, split hot crackers with a knife and bake cracker halves for 4 to 6 minutes more or till golden brown. Cool. Wrap to store. Makes about 36.

Nutrition Analysis Chart

Use these analyses to compare nutritional values of different recipes. This information was calculated using Agriculture Handbook Number 8, published by the United States Department of Agriculture, as the primary source.

In compiling the nutrition analyses, we made the following assumptions:

- For all of the soup and stew recipes made with meat, the nutrition analyses were calculated using weights or measures for cooked meat.
- Garnishes and optional ingredients were not included in the nutrition analyses.
- When two ingredient options appear in a recipe, calculations were made using the first one.
- For ingredients of variable weight (such as "2½- to 3-pound broiler-fryer chicken") or for recipes with a serving range ("Makes 4 to 6 servings"), calculations were made using the first figure.

	Per Serving						Percent U.S. RDA Per Serving							
	Calories	Protein (g)	Carbohydrate (g)	Fat (g)	Sodium (mg)	Potassium (mg)	Protein	Vitamin A	Vitamin C	Thiamine	Riboflavin	Niacin	Calcium	Iron
Main-Dish Soups														
Autumn Beef Stew (p. 94)	330	18	35	13	658	680	30	6	30	15	10	20	6	20
Barley-Beef Soup (p. 57)	380	28	35	10	870	540	45	2	50	10	15	30	4	25
Beef and Lentil Soup (p. 55)	230	19	31	4	800	760	30	20	33	15	10	15	6	25
Beef and Zucchini Stew with Cheese Dumplings (p. 101)	480	27	38	25	1060	830	40	25	50	25	25	30	30	30
Beefy Vegetable Soup (p. 52)	260	22	29	6	740	610	35	80	30	15	10	20	6	25
Bratwurst-Macaroni Soup (p. 11)	527	27	55	22	2105	729	42	15	6	64	45	31	38	22
Carbonnade-Style Beef Soup (p. 54)	380	28	38	9	910	730	45	0	35	15	20	35	6	25
Cauliflower Crab-Chowder (p. 86)	370	18	18	25	768	520	30	50	67	15	20	10	20	10
Cheese-Bean Chowder (p. 73)	424	27	43	17	1034	845	41	16	5	36	26	7	49	22
Chicken and Vegetable Stew (p. 66)	280	27	29	6	680	980	40	25	70	15	15	50	4	15
Chicken Stew with Potato Dumplings (p. 100)	301	27	31	7	811	654	41	82	21	21	19	49	8	19
Chicken Wonton Soup (p. 67)	200	23	14	6	1150	490	35	130	90	10	20	40	4	10
Chorizo Chili (p. 76)	530	37	25	32	1040	660	60	60	270	40	30	40	25	35
Corn and Broccoli Chowder (p. 8)	340	27	32	13	1970	650	40	40	60	35	30	20	35	15
Corn-Pasta Chowder (p. 20)	440	21	66	12	1300	760	35	10	17	40	35	25	35	10
Country-Style Pork Stew (p. 90)	280	21	17	14	510	780	30	20	34	45	20	20	10	15
Cream of Artichoke and Fish Chowder (p. 48)	310	18	10	23	380	540	30	120	12	8	15	15	6	4
Creamy Northern Bean Soup (p. 72)	320	21	56	3	490	1120	30	140	30	40	20	10	25	35
Creamy Taco Soup (p. 85)	440	26	24	27	707	640	40	20	16	15	25	20	30	20
Curried Chicken-Rice Soup (p. 66)	420	32	53	9	1200	810	50	210	18	20	15	50	8	20
Elegant Chicken and Asparagus Soup (p. 84)	380	25	12	26	313	460	40	30	28	15	20	40	10	10
Elegant Oyster Stew (p. 60)	670	24	38	47	380	1000	35	35	83	25	30	20	30	60

	Per Serving						Percent U.S. RDA Per Serving							
	Calories	Protein (g)	Carbohydrate (g)	Fat (g)	Sodium (mg)	Potassium (mg)	Protein	Vitamin A	Vitamin C	Thiamine	Riboflavin	Niacin	Calcium	Iron
Main-Dish Soups *(continued)*														
Fish and Rice Soup (p. 49)	230	23	28	1	952	920	35	25	61	15	6	20	4	10
Fish and Spinach Chowder (p. 49)	250	24	21	8	623	900	35	30	35	8	20	10	30	10
Fish-Succotash Chowder (p. 48)	360	27	27	16	749	650	40	15	10	15	10	15	8	10
Gumbo (p. 108)	580	32	39	33	1215	710	50	6	33	45	15	30	10	20
Ham and Rice Soup (p. 54)	170	16	16	4	1050	400	25	4	35	40	8	20	2	10
Hot and Sour Parsnip Soup (p. 42)	230	17	22	9	1133	550	25	0	11	15	15	10	25	25
Hot and Spicy Chili (p. 78)	290	25	32	8	970	1170	40	50	55	20	15	30	10	35
Hot Tamale Stew (p. 11)	430	22	47	18	1110	700	35	45	55	10	25	25	35	40
Indonesian-Style Chicken Chowder (p. 21)	440	24	37	21	610	590	35	15	4	25	35	30	35	10
Lamb and Garbanzo Stew (p. 93)	340	26	27	14	720	910	40	20	28	20	20	35	10	30
Lamb-Sausage Soup (p. 57)	470	31	20	30	630	750	50	120	23	30	25	35	10	20
Lamb Stew with Curried Cornmeal Dumplings (p. 98)	410	23	31	22	700	510	35	8	20	25	30	35	10	20
Lima-Broccoli Soup (p. 72)	200	13	25	6	710	770	20	10	30	15	10	15	6	20
Manhattan Clam Chowder (p. 61)	238	14	24	119	1375	1025	21	131	89	15	14	20	12	38
Meatball Soup (p. 112)	280	24	15	14	1200	620	35	40	33	15	25	25	25	20
Mideastern Lamb Stew (p. 93)	400	23	48	15	727	930	35	25	85	30	20	30	8	25
New England Clam Chowder (p. 60)	610	20	32	45	1080	1030	30	30	45	15	25	20	25	40
Oriental-Style Chicken Stew (p. 92)	390	21	47	10	686	610	35	50	122	25	25	45	4	20
Oven Beef Stew (p. 92)	340	20	32	15	426	840	30	210	45	20	10	25	4	25
Pork and Cabbage Stew with Dumplings (p. 100)	440	23	49	17	640	880	35	420	42	60	25	30	10	20
Sausage-Bean Soup (p. 10)	340	15	25	20	1100	520	25	70	8	25	10	15	8	15
Sausage-Cheese Chowder (p. 82)	570	24	19	44	1310	600	35	130	30	30	30	15	45	10
Sausage-Navy Bean Stew (p. 73)	550	29	55	25	1176	1400	45	10	50	70	20	25	15	45
Seafood Chowder (p. 46)	190	28	16	2	951	1130	45	160	35	10	10	20	8	15
Short Rib-Sauerkraut Soup (p. 55)	320	21	18	18	1450	790	30	0	36	10	10	20	6	25
Snappy Tomato-Veal Stew (p. 94)	300	20	30	12	860	1100	30	45	90	15	20	30	6	20
Speedy Pastrami Chili (p. 10)	420	18	40	21	2240	1040	25	50	10	8	15	15	10	25
Spicy Split Pea Soup (p. 43)	350	21	65	1	644	1030	30	150	49	45	15	20	6	30
Texas-Style Chili (p. 78)	320	30	22	12	320	640	45	15	2	20	15	25	4	25
Three-Bean Chili-Beer Soup (p. 79)	410	25	35	17	510	930	40	35	81	20	20	30	10	35
Tuna-Corn Chowder (p. 85)	330	25	29	12	628	540	40	20	9	10	20	50	15	10
Tuna-Rosemary Soup (p. 21)	210	22	27	1	910	340	35	6	10	20	10	50	4	15
Turkey Chili with Pasta (p. 79)	450	47	38	12	690	1160	70	45	32	25	30	50	25	35
Turkey Tortellini Soup (p. 67)	220	30	12	6	530	470	45	10	25	10	20	20	10	20
Turkey Vegetable Soup (p. 64)	160	24	11	2	640	640	35	290	71	8	15	25	8	15
Veal Stew with Pastry Topper (p. 104)	920	40	59	55	650	810	60	220	18	40	50	60	10	50
Side-Dish Soups														
Apple-Cot Fruit Soup (p. 30)	150	1	40	0	20	390	0	30	25	0	2	4	0	6
Beef Stock (p. 34)	0	0	0	0	400	0	0	0	0	0	0	0	0	0
Borscht (p. 42)	130	4	23	4	744	720	4	110	60	8	6	6	8	10
Carrot-Barley Chowder (p. 43)	320	7	39	16	462	730	10	290	40	10	10	10	15	10
Chicken Stock (p. 36)	0	0	0	0	306	0	0	0	0	0	0	0	0	0
Chili-Bean Pasta Soup (p. 20)	140	7	27	1	320	410	10	10	15	10	6	10	4	10

	Per Serving						Percent U.S. RDA Per Serving							
	Calories	Protein (g)	Carbohydrate (g)	Fat (g)	Sodium (mg)	Potassium (mg)	Protein	Vitamin A	Vitamin C	Thiamine	Riboflavin	Niacin	Calcium	Iron
Side-Dish Soups *(continued)*														
Chilled Zucchini Soup (p. 26)	150	4	11	10	330	490	6	120	20	6	8	10	6	4
Cream of Potato Soup (p. 85)	260	7	28	14	375	680	10	15	50	10	15	8	15	6
Cream of Tomato Soup (p. 84)	310	12	31	17	850	990	20	60	45	20	30	10	35	10
Creamy Broccoli Soup (p. 27)	150	4	12	10	690	270	6	30	30	4	6	2	10	4
Curried Creamy Carrot Soup (p. 27)	180	8	17	10	610	640	10	650	15	10	15	15	15	8
Dilly Green Pea Soup (p. 26)	250	10	17	16	570	370	15	25	20	20	15	20	10	10
Fish Stock (p. 36)	0	0	0	0	180	0	0	0	0	0	0	0	0	0
Gazpacho (p. 14)	60	2	11	2	480	460	2	40	90	8	4	6	2	6
Guacamole Soup (p. 15)	110	3	5	9	330	135	4	8	12	0	4	4	4	0
Ham-and-Spinach Soup (p. 19)	150	11	20	3	730	370	20	50	20	30	10	15	4	10
Lentil-Pumpkin Soup (p. 26)	90	5	16	2	410	340	8	360	6	4	8	2	10	10
Lima-Sesame Soup (p. 70)	130	5	16	4	463	480	8	120	20	10	4	4	4	10
Minestrone (p. 40)	130	7	25	1	420	540	10	60	40	10	6	8	8	10
Mixed Fruit Soup (p. 30)	150	1	38	0	10	330	0	8	2	0	0	0	0	4
Pick-a-Pasta Soup (p. 18)	120	4	24	1	370	95	6	0	0	15	6	8	2	6
Pea Pod Appetizer Broth (p. 21)	100	4	20	1	540	110	6	0	8	15	6	8	2	6
Pepperoni and Vegetable Soup (p. 20)	190	8	21	8	780	300	10	50	20	15	10	10	4	8
Speedy Borscht (p. 42)	120	4	21	4	1094	620	6	150	30	6	10	4	10	15
Veal Stock (p. 37)	0	0	0	0	180	0	0	0	0	0	0	0	0	0
Vegetable Stock (p. 37)	0	0	0	0	330	0	0	0	0	0	0	0	0	0
Vichyssoise (p. 24)	190	6	19	10	490	660	8	6	20	6	8	15	6	6
Wild-Rice Soup (p. 86)	210	7	22	11	283	310	10	15	6	10	20	6	15	6
Miscellaneous														
Apple Dumplings with Raspberry Sauce (p. 117)	510	5	78	22	150	240	6	2	27	20	10	10	2	10
Bibb Lettuce with Creamy Italian Dressing (p. 115)	280	2	6	28	340	280	2	20	10	4	4	0	6	2
Bran Batter Bread (p. 116)	140	5	25	3	200	150	8	2	0	15	10	8	4	10
Cheese Popcorn (p. 119)	25	1	2	2	30	5	0	0	0	0	0	0	0	0
Cheese Wafers (p. 120)	25	1	2	2	50	10	0	0	0	0	0	0	0	0
Cheesy Garlic Crisps (p. 119)	40	1	4	2	80	10	0	0	0	0	0	0	2	0
Chili Popcorn (p. 119)	20	0	2	2	15	10	0	2	0	0	0	0	0	0
Crusty Onion Rolls (p. 116)	150	4	28	3	230	55	6	0	0	15	10	10	0	8
Garlic Crisps (p. 119)	35	1	4	2	60	10	0	0	0	0	0	0	0	0
Garlic Popcorn (p. 119)	20	0	2	2	45	5	0	0	0	0	0	0	0	0
Herbed Croutons (p. 118)	60	1	6	4	115	15	0	2	0	2	0	0	0	2
Herbed Popcorn (p. 119)	20	0	2	2	15	5	0	0	0	0	0	0	0	0
Onion Popcorn (p. 119)	20	0	2	2	65	5	0	0	0	0	0	0	0	0
Potato and Rye Bread (p. 115)	80	2	15	1	115	65	2	0	2	6	4	4	0	4
Presto! It's Pesto! (p. 43)	80	2	1	7	95	55	2	25	8	0	0	0	4	2
Seeded Rye Crackers (p. 120)	35	1	5	1	20	10	0	0	0	2	0	0	0	0
Surprising Spaetzle (p. 101)	150	6	25	2	300	95	8	2	0	15	10	8	4	8
Yeast Crackers (p. 121)	40	1	5	1	35	10	0	0	0	2	2	2	0	0

A–B

C–E

F–N

O–R

S–Z

Tips